Jesus Christ is the same yesterday, today, and fore[...] business of bringing deliverance and freedom to the[...] Dr. Ernie Sauve provides a biblically sound framework for deliverance ministry. His insights are practical, Christ-centered, and sensitive to the leading of the Holy Spirit. I highly recommend *The Freedom Manual - Deliverance and Inner Healing from Start to Finish* for any believer who desires to partner with God's desire to bring lasting freedom to His sons and daughters!

Dr. Ché Ahn
President, Harvest International Ministry
Senior Leader, Harvest Rock Church, Pasadena, CA
International Chancellor, Wagner University

I highly recommend Dr. Ernie Sauve, Jr.'s new book, *The Freedom Manual – Deliverance and Inner Healing from Start to Finish* for deliverance practitioners and individual believers that want to walk in freedom. This is a detailed and precise "how to manual" for the deliverance ministry. Dr Ernie takes the uncertainty and perplexity out of the deliverance process. Each chapter provides significant steps to bring about successful outcomes. We are experiencing the beginning of a great move of God and one of the most important aspects of this move is deliverance, which is the Children's Bread. I have personally seen many lives changed through the effective deliverance and healing ministry and writings of Dr. Sauve. This is a must have manual for anyone involved in the deliverance ministry.

Apostle Mario Bramnick
New Wine Ministries Church

The Freedom Manual – Deliverance and Inner Healing from Start to Finish is a well written and useful tool for all deliverance and inner healing practitioners. Dr. Ernie and Silvia present the ministry of deliverance in a way that empowers the practitioner to be successful, understand the theology that supports deliverance, as well imparting the essential tools. This manual is a must have for any healing leader.

Dr. Rob Covell
Chief Academic Officer, Wagner University

The ministry of Jesus was characterized by His teaching on the Kingdom of God and the demonstration of the Kingdom by casting out demons and healing the sick. He entrusted His disciples with the same task. Today however, most Christians have no idea where to start nor what to do with demon oppression and harassment. God's timing is perfect! *The Freedom Manual – Deliverance and Inner Healing from Start to Finish* is what every believer needs to set up deliverance sessions and minister effectively to those held captive by the enemy. I really believe in the process the authors have outlined in this prophetic manual which includes a Truth, Power, and a Healing Encounter. The Truth Encounter brings revelation from Heaven that unlock God's amazing love and goodness. Dr. Ernie and Silvia will take you step by step through the process while at the same time allowing Holy Spirit to lead the way. Thank you, Ernie and Silvia, for being obedient to the Lord in writing this powerful manual.

Pasqual Urrabazo
Apostle – Kingdom Harvest Alliance

THE FREEDOM MANUAL

DELIVERANCE AND INNER HEALING FROM START TO FINISH

Dr. Ernie and Silvia Sauve

© Copyright 2023 – DayStream Ministries International
July 4, 2023

Published by DayStream Ministries International
P.O. Box 5261
Lighthouse Point, Florida
33074

All rights reserved. No part of this publication may be reproduced, stored in a retrieval system, or transmitted in any form or by any means – for example, electronic, photocopy, recording – without the prior written permission by the publisher. The only exception is brief quotations in printed reviews.

ISBN 978-0-9964302-9-6

Unless otherwise noted, all Bible references are Scripture taken from the New King James Version®. Copyright © 1982 by Thomas Nelson, Inc. Used by permission. All rights reserved.

Cover design by Delvis Martínez

Note from the publisher:
This manual, *The Freedom Manual – Deliverance and Inner Healing from Start to Finish*, is not intended to provide any medical or psychological advice. The information presented herein is biblical, pastoral, and spiritual in nature. It is not professional, clinical, or medical counsel and should not be considered as such. The authors, Dr. Ernie and Silvia Sauve, together with Daystream Ministries International hereby disclaim any and all liability for any adverse or damaging effects that may be asserted or claimed to have arisen as a result of the use of this manual.

Printed in the U.S.A

Dedication

This manual is dedicated to my wonderful wife, Silvia, who has stood with me in the deliverance ministry. We have been together in every session; she has amazing discernment along with a wealth of experience and understanding of the subject. Together we have developed the system I have presented in this volume.

This manual is dedicated to deliverance ministers. It is for the caring and loving individuals who, with fiery passion, hate all the destructive works of the enemy. Yours is a priceless and exceptional motivation, sometimes underestimated in its potential, and often underutilized in the Body of Christ. The Holy Spirit is now preparing up-and-coming deliverance ministers who may have been unaware of their untapped potential. Be encouraged, it will soon be revealed. We are praying for you.

This manual is dedicated to all those who are on a personal quest for freedom and healing. Perhaps you have suffered sleepless nights and days filled with anxiety and fear. For too long you have endured demonic affliction and harassment without being able to break the cycles of bondage. You understand that the Bible contains truths about a quality of life and relationship with God that far surpasses your own experience. Our prayer is that this volume will connect you with the healing virtue of Jesus for past hurts and trauma, bring you to the place of dealing with all the lies of the enemy and provide freedom and authority to dislodge all demonic entities from your life. This manual is for you, a tool for your freedom and a bridge to the abundant life in Christ. We are praying for you.

> The Spirit of the Lord God *is* upon Me,
> Because the Lord has anointed Me
> To preach good tidings to the poor;
> He has sent Me to heal the brokenhearted,
> To proclaim liberty to the captives,
> And the opening of the prison to *those who are* bound...
> Isaiah 61:1

Dr. Ernie Sauve Jr.

Contents

Foreword ix
Testimony xiii
Introduction. 1
Action Steps 8
Preparing for the Session 9
Prayers of Release. 16
The Day of the Session. 33
Deliverance Prayer 35
Forgiveness and Inner Healing. 37
Breaking Soul Ties 41
Terminating Generational Curses. 43
Revoking Agreement with Darkness. 49
Demolishing Strongholds 52
Evicting Demons 86
Blessing. 89
Homework 91
Follow Up 93
Moving Forward 96

Appendix A: Confidential Questionnaire. 97
Appendix B: Request and Consent to Receive In-Depth Personal Ministry 117
Appendix C: Deliverance Preparation Checklist 120
Appendix D: The Session Checklist 121
Appendix E: Additional Prayers of Release. 122
Appendix F: Building a Team. 126
DayStream Information and Tools 129

Foreword

Cindy is a very talented teenager who excels in the arts and music. Unfortunately, her father was a very controlling man gripped by addictions and violence. Even though he served in a city role of protecting the public, he himself was not practicing this in his home. Eventually, his bad behaviors and addictions caught up with him outside the home. He broke the law, lost his job, and paid for his crimes.

He left home while Cindy was a toddler. Basically, she was raised without his negative influence inside the home. But when there is a strong repeated generational pattern that the enemy establishes, even children who are not in the presence of a parent gripped by darkness can and often do experience the same bondage. Why? Because Satan and his army are legalists and, in their attempt to keep a demonic hold will continue to attach themselves with their evil agendas and bondages until the generational curses and soul ties are broken and under the blood of Jesus.

In her younger years, Cindy was drawn like a magnet to drinking and drugs. It was as if a desire and compulsion deep within her drew her to this lifestyle. She was lured into addictions and every trap the enemy could set in order to ensure her drug abuse and drug addiction was set into play in her life from a young age. One thing we must understand is the enemy and his army of darkness do not want children to know or understand the love of our heavenly Father. Our foe will perpetuate lies and cause hurtful situations to set the trap of bondage.

One evening following the service, Cindy made her way to the altar. You could see the torment and hurt in this young girl's life. I quickly made my way to her and began to minister freedom out of the tangible presence of the Father's heart of love. Soon, I began to receive prophetic revelation concerning her abusive and absent father and the severe harm this generational curse was causing her. I knew we had to break the generational curse of the stronghold of bondage to addictions between she and her father, but I also knew that the Lord wanted to bless her with His father's heart to pave the way for her freedom. I asked a man in the church who functions in the role of her spiritual father to do a healing act. He stood as a male figure in her life and repented to her on behalf of men, her father, and the fatherlessness that had followed her throughout her entire life. He repented for the violence, neglect, and drug addictions that a man, her father, had allowed into her life.

Cindy began to weep as the genuine love of her spiritual and heavenly Father flowed through this man to her. He wept as he began to tell her how beautiful she is and how proud he is of her. I will never forget these words as tears streamed down his face, "Cindy, you are beautiful. I am so proud of you. God has amazing things in store for you. I believe in you. These issues with your father in the past no longer have to hold you. Tonight, is the night to let this go and receive your freedom."

You see, Cindy truly had desired freedom from drugs and alcohol. And she would be able to keep herself free for a period of time, but soon she would fall back into the trap of this bondage again. Cindy had truly forgiven her father as well, but this generational curse and the unholy soul tie between she and her father continued to pull her back into the demonic cycle of addiction. After, her spiritual father prayed, I stepped in and began to break the generational curse of bondage, addiction, violence, neglect, and fatherlessness. I severed the unholy soul ties between she and her father and his generations all the way back to Adam and Eve.

Cindy began to receive amazing freedom and was literally transforming in front of our eyes. Her countenance changed. Her cheek color went from pale white to rosy pink. Her sadness soon turned to joy, and she was smiling and laughing at the goodness, love, and freedom the Lord had brought to her. Now Cindy had other issues that the Lord needed to touch on in the near future to bring her complete freedom, but from that night the drugs, alcohol, and addictive behavior totally left her. Cindy has not been drawn or pulled back in since that evening.

What a beautiful testimony of deliverance and freedom! A Biblical text that comes to mind when sharing Cindy's deliverance testimony is Acts 10:38, *"God anointed Jesus of Nazareth with the Holy Spirit and with power, who went about doing good and healing all who were oppressed by the devil, for God was with Him."* Today and in this strategic time, God is raising up His ministers with the same anointing! I can't remember a time when deliverance and inner healing is on the forefront as it is today. From movie theaters to denominational churches to university campuses; its literally everywhere you turn.

Therefore, the need for a balanced, biblical, and effective system that embraces Kingdom values and Holy Spirit empowerment is so vital. Dr. Ernie and Silvia are uniquely positioned for such a time as this with their pastoral approach to deliverance and inner healing. They have tapped into the mantle of those who have gone before them in this much needed ministry and in this manual bring an updated and fresh expression for both the deliverance practitioner and those who seek self-deliverance. They have captured the essence of the classic power encounter and added a truth encounter component with conversation and prayer that exposes darkness and brings alignment with the King.

There is a wealth of experience between the lines of this manual. Deliverance and inner healing are simple once there is experience in the field and close connection with Holy Spirit. Patience, love, and time are necessary to walk an oppressed individual carefully through the steps to eliminate demonic harassment and spiritual contamination that built the strongholds. The authority delegated to the Kingdom minded Christian combined with a practical understanding of how demons attack, enter and harass an individual will bring the intended result, demons will leave, and deep healing will occur! It is a beautiful thing to see a life transformed by the power of God!

The following is a powerful testimony from Lisa.

> For years I struggled with fear. It wasn't a fear of leaving the house or speaking in public; the typical fears one would think of when they hear the word fear.
>
> This was a fear of my husband cheating on me. I struggled with this fear for most of my marriage even though my husband had never cheated on me or done anything to betray me in any way. I would entertain a thought in my head of, "What if my husband cheated on me." That thought turned into another thought and before I knew it, I really believed he was being unfaithful. I was gripped with fear, and it caused a lot of anxiety and depression in me. It took a toll on our marriage as well because my husband had this wife who didn't trust him.
>
> I was in bondage and no matter how much I read scripture and prayed I couldn't get the deliverance I needed to be set free. I needed guidance on how to do this, but I was embarrassed to even talk to anybody about it and ask for prayer, so I suffered for years. I knew I couldn't go on living this way, so I went to Becca and her team. I finally received the deliverance and healing from God that I had prayed for. One key spiritual

practice I learned is that I had to take those thoughts captive like the Word of God says.

The thoughts would try to enter from time to time but I would immediately take those thoughts captive and say out loud, "My husband loves me. He is faithful to me. I refuse to listen to the lies of the enemy." I also had to be conscious of what I watched on television and read. I couldn't allow television shows, radio programs or articles that dealt with infidelity as entertainment to put ideas in my mind.

Praise God for Lisa's freedom! Friends, the Word of God is clear that we do not battle against flesh and blood but against powers of darkness (Eph. 6:12). It is our kingdom inheritance to live a life delivered from strongholds and walk in victorious freedom. And as clearly stated by Jesus, "These signs will accompany those who have believed, in my name they will cast out demons..." (Mark 16:17). In *The Freedom Manual – Deliverance and Inner Healing from Start to Finish*, Dr. Ernie and Silvia Sauve have mapped out a practical, strategic, and effective tool for all called to cast out demons and see captives set free. This manual is a must have in the arsenal for every believer functioning in the kingdom call of deliverance ministry.

Rebecca Greenwood
Cofounder – Christian Harvest International
Strategic Prayer Apostolic Network
International Freedom Group

Testimony

I accepted Jesus Christ as my Lord and Savior in 1980. I went into full time ministry in 1989. I am a pastor and have operated in the prophetic gifting. I have seen the Lord do many miracles including opening blind eyes and have participated in typical deliverance meetings from time to time.

Then the Lord gave me a dream not long ago that there were open doors in my house. A few nights later, I was sitting by my pool to spend time with the Lord. He spoke very clearly to me to go read Ernie's book "Deliverance on Purpose." In this book Ernie talks about how we "open doors" to demonic activities in our lives. This got my attention, and I took the process seriously. Throughout the process, it was amazing how the Lord revealed areas in my life and my ancestry that allowed the devil a stronghold in my life.

During my session with Ernie and Silvia I was amazed at the things I saw coming out of myself! Ernie's prophetic insight and Silvia's words of knowledge hit the bullseye time after time. The Lord used them so powerfully! I feel so free and have a sensitivity to sin that I have never had. I am so thankful to the Lord, and to Ernie and Silvia, for this process. You won't regret going through all the steps. I only wish I had done this 40 years ago.

- A Pastor

Introduction

This might come as a surprise for some, but demons are not the problem. In deliverance and inner healing, the focus is not on demons. The emphasis is on Jesus who is in the business of bringing people who are in bondage and under oppression of the enemy into the spiritual victory and freedom. The emphasis is on healing the internal brokenness and vulnerability, closing the doors to the enemy, and removing the legal rights demons claim to have. This involves a uniquely designed method outlined here as a simple, step by step process that points to a partnership with the Holy Spirit to bring freedom and healing on every level of human experience. It is our prayer that you will be empowered and emboldened to walk in freedom and set the captives free.

The perceived importance of deliverance ministry is on the upswing! In recent months, there have been a surge of appointment requests and deliverance ministers have a waiting list, sometimes a very long one! Quite possibly there are more people than ever sensing a need to break demonic patterns and oppression in a quest for freedom. My question is: what are you going to do when you are asked to minister to someone in need of deliverance and inner healing?

There is a lot of confusion and misunderstanding regarding just how a deliverance session should be handled. Unprepared deliverance ministers tend to overly trust their own level of discernment, to lean heavily on improvisation, and to be reluctant to use a system. Our desire is constant growth towards maturity, effectiveness, and professionalism as practitioners of deliverance and healing.

The system outlined in this book has been proven through years of application to be safe, effective, and biblical. Having said that, we must be very careful to always seek God's specific guidance for every deliverance session. There is no substitute for the supernatural ministry of the Holy Spirit.

This manual is designed to be a step-by-step overview and start-to-finish guide for the deliverance process. The approach is from a what-to-do-next perspective, and it looks to simplify and breakdown a potentially complex process in a way that is easy to understand and to apply. It is designed to enhance our discernment by giving the Holy Spirit a greater opportunity to interact with us in the heat of battle that is the deliverance session.

Whether you are an experienced deliverance and inner healing practitioner or a Christian seeking a self-deliverance method, this manual is for you.

The purpose of this manual then is to:

- Demystify the deliverance process.
- Simplify the system.
- Help Christians in their self-deliverance process.
- Allow ministers to easily replicate functional procedures.
- Recruit, train, activate and release more deliverance ministers.
- Leave the reader with the conviction "I can do this!"

The effective use of this manual requires a thorough understanding and personal application of the areas addressed herein. Having only theoretical understanding of the harassment of the lies of the enemy, will not be enough. The practitioner must learn the subject matter, apply it diligently to personal life and quite possibly should go through the process personally!

The hard part of deliverance and healing is finished! The death of Jesus on the cross of Calvary and His shed blood provide for redemption, forgiveness, deliverance, and healing. It's our time to walk in freedom and help others come into the fullness God has for them by enforcing that victory in their areas of brokenness. The fact that you have this book in your hands shows that your personal process in the Lord has brought you to the place of wanting freedom, helping others as well. You know the Word, and you have a testimony of God's power and intervention in your life. It's time to move forward and implement the action plan. So many people are waiting for their spiritual and emotional freedom. Let's do it. God is with you!

What is deliverance?

Today outside of the context of biblical deliverance and healing, when given the option to move away from pain or move toward pleasure, people will normally choose relief of their pain. The desperate situation they find themselves in, prompts a search for the way to quick symptomatic relief. If Jesus is not in the mix, invariably the "relief" spells greater oppression and suffering. Addictive tendencies and mood-altering habits are developed as suffering must be mitigated. Relief with food, alcohol or substance abuse, sexual relations, or pornography to mention just a few. All these open doors to demons and establishes legal rights for the enemy to cause torment. So, the cycle of pain and addiction continues and the demonic solidifies its presence producing strongholds of the soul. This dynamic occurs in the life of believers and non-believers.

Deliverance is a two-part activity.

The first part is removal.

1. Closing open doors to the enemy.
2. Removing legal rights of the enemy.
3. Healing the wounds that increase vulnerability to the enemy.
4. Breaking the lies of the enemy that hinder, harass, and block a person from fullness in Christ.
5. Dismantling strongholds.
6. Breaking cyclical patterns of sinful behavior that hold people back from their God-given purpose.
7. Casting out demons.

The second part replacement

1. We open doors and communication with the Lord in three dimensions: Father, Son and, Holy Spirit.
2. We establish covenant of love and obedience with the Lord.
3. We establish God's truth to replace the darkness of the past.
4. We establish new thought patterns that replace the old.
5. We help establish new biblical patterns that usher in God's blessings in a tangible way.

6. We pray in an encounter with the Lord.

7. We declare blessings to empower the new post-deliverance life.

Parallel Biblical Ministry Concepts

The activity of deliverance and inner healing are now defined. Now we must go on to introduce biblical concepts that are closely related and a vital part of the overall process.

1. Sanctification – The enemy knows how to exploit the damaged soul by prodding, provoking, and harassing a person's life before Christ. This leads to an endless, and needless state of internal conflict that form strongholds and grant legal rights to the enemy. Sanctification in key areas will close the enemy's access to the soul.

2. Renewing the mind – Every aspect of the process we use will assist the prayee in the development of a healthy mindset based on biblical truth.

3. Discipleship – We firmly believe that a deliverance component must be in place in every church so the new believer can quickly overcome the destructive patterns of the past life. Discipleship must include deliverance and inner healing.

4. Spiritual Maturity – A wholistic approach must be considered here as spiritual maturity is part of the whole spirit – soul – body of the individual. Frequently spiritual maturity is defined as faithfulness in church attendance and a conceptual understanding of biblical principles only. There can be no true spiritual maturity without the body and the soul lining up with the Word. Immaturity for the Christian may be expressed by the lack of Christlikeness, the behavior and lifestyle of one who does not know the Lord. The result being that the person lives as a "slave" under the oppression and deception of the enemy.

5. Pastoral Ministry – The traditional role of the pastor is to lead, feed and guide a congregation with the Word of God. We believe that pastoral ministry deals with every area of a person's life including breaking demonic lies, darkness, and destructive behavior that forms strongholds. In other words, pastoral ministry must include deliverance and inner healing.

6. Accountability – Post session counseling must include accountability as the prayee may still be weak and vulnerable to spiritual attack.

7. Counseling – There is a counseling component to the deliverance process. People come to us with tangled emotions and a series of complicated life situations that need to be addressed. Quietly suffering as they have not found trustworthy confidants to release their pain and lead the way into wholeness.

8. Correction – Often left out of Christian ministry altogether, correction points out the connection between ungodly behavior and the resulting oppression and destruction from the enemy. This will eliminate the cause of sinful behavior and outline the path of repentance and restoration. 2 Timothy 2:25-26

We can outline several objectives in our deliverance process to help the prayee:

- Discover the real problem areas.
- Uncover generational iniquity.
- Identify personal sin and lead into repentance.
- Receive healing of trauma and emotional wounds.
- Close doors and remove legal rights of the enemy.
- Cast out demonic intruders.
- Establish a clear path for personal victory by renewing the mind.
- Develop a new Christlike lifestyle with personal discipline.

The process outlined in this manual can be reduced to 3 main areas:

1. The Truth Encounter – Revelation from the Holy Spirit will demolish the lies of the enemy and bring supernatural joy in understanding God's truth.

2. The Power Encounter – God's presence displaces darkness and destroys strongholds. Demons will have no option other than to leave.

3. The Healing Encounter – The healing virtue of Jesus flows into the damaged areas of the soul. Pain embedded in traumatic memories is removed and the heart is healed, internal brokenness is restored.

What is the desired outcome of the deliverance ministry?

The deliverance and inner healing sessions have a desired outcome. This ministry will have a lasting impact on the person in every area of life. The deliverance process is designed to be a transformational event and process.

- Spiritual maturity will be noticed in all areas of the person's life: spirit, soul, and body.

- Relationships will come into divine order: family, church, and friendships.

- Professional development: When the blinders have been removed and the lies of the enemy destroyed, growth and financial blessings are a natural result.

- Active participation, service, and commitment in the Kingdom and the local church.

- Purpose and destiny are seen in the light of God's design and equipping. You are created with a purpose.

- Joy, a sense of personal freedom and fulfillment.

This manual is designed to be a diagnostic tool to help pinpoint specific areas of need in the life of the prayee. With the power of the Holy Spirit, you, the deliverance and inner healing practitioner, will help enforce the victory of Jesus over all forms of darkness. With experience and increased discernment, you are well equipped to minister effectively and powerfully. Immediate results will be seen but the real impact will be generational blessings and a legacy of Kingdom alignment and impact. Yours is a high calling, be bold in this extremely important ministry.

We honor the legacy of Dr. Peter Wagner and his amazing wife Doris. Their impact in the areas of spiritual warfare, intercession, deliverance, and inner healing shaped our lives through their direct teaching, seminars, and books. Our DNA is a result of our education and studies at Wagner University that Dr. Peter founded in 1998.

We also honor the legacy of Dr. Bill Sudduth, known as a pillar in the deliverance ministry, who personally mentored us for over 10 years.

> And Jesus went about all Galilee, teaching in their synagogues, preaching the gospel of the kingdom, and healing all kinds of sickness and all kinds of disease among the people. Then His fame went throughout all Syria; and they brought to Him all sick people who were afflicted with various diseases and torments, and those who were demon-possessed, epileptics, and paralytics; and He healed them. Matthew 4:23-24

Dr. Ernie and Silvia Sauve

Action Steps

This section outlines the general flow of the typical deliverance process. If you are a deliverance practitioner there is flexibility to follow the Holy Spirit with steps 2 – 9. If you are using this manual for self-deliverance, follow steps 1 – 9 in order.

1. Preparing for the Session.
2. Prayers of Release.
3. Deliverance Prayer.
4. Forgiveness.
5. Inner Healing.
6. Breaking Soul Ties.
7. Dealing with Generational Curses.
8. Breaking Agreement with Darkness.
9. Evicting demonic intruders.
10. Blessing.
11. Assign homework.
12. Follow up.

Preparing for the Session

Preparing for the Session Overview

- Initial contact and determination if deliverance is needed.
- Assign pre-deliverance homework.
- Prayee signs consent form and fills out the questionnaire.
- Prayers of release.
- Plan the date of the session.

Is Deliverance Needed?

How will we know if deliverance and inner healing sessions are needed? People come with life situations that are beyond their control: their relationships are breaking up, their thought life is perverted or bizarre, they are under a constant barrage of the enemy's attack, they have coping mechanisms and addictive tendencies, they see demons in their house or in their dreams, they sense that darkness is dragging them down, and more. Let me suggest a few common issues to help discern the need for personal deliverance.

- Difficulty with anger management.
- Problems with physical violence and aggressive behavior.
- An invisible barrier that blocks getting ahead in life.
- Habitually telling lies and feeling little remorse.
- Past hurts and traumatic memories plaguing the mind continually.
- Difficulty with forgiving the perpetrators of offense and trauma.
- Personal involvement in the occult, witchcraft, or Freemasonry.
- Difficulty accepting the Bible as God's word.

- Pervasive feeling that God is a distant reality.
- Struggling with addictions and escape experiences for years.
- Overeating when nervous, unhappy, or depressed.
- Feeling overwhelmed with life circumstances.
- An adulterous affair and tendency to be easily flirtatious.
- Fear of being truly being known for who you are.
- Having a secret life that no one knows about.
- Struggling with addictive tendencies such as food, sex, pornography, alcohol, or drugs.
- Fearing that everything is falling apart.
- Cyclical patterns and behavior that cannot be broken.
- Having father issues: abuse, abandonment, or rejection.
- Experiencing sexual encounters at night that can't be stopped or avoided.
- Fearing to know for sure just what happened in the past.

Once there is a clear understanding with the local church leadership regarding guidelines, and once the team has been defined and is developing, it is time to move forward. Please realize that this is a work in progress. You will define, redefine, and improve along the way. Begin as soon as possible to prepare people for their session. The waters will open before you as you walk forward to take the land. The authority of the Kingdom that Jesus promised to His disciples is yours today: receive it, apply it, and work it for the benefit of those God sends your way.

The Prayee Must Be Prepared

Many people are looking for a quick fix for the issues that have been plaguing them for years; however, there must be a proactive role in the process. Conviction from the Holy Spirit is not instantaneous, so preparation ahead of the deliverance process is key. This preparation engages the person in the individual quest for freedom and transformation.

Failure to prepare a person for the deliverance process is one of the primary reasons for an unsuccessful outcome. As deliverance ministers, we don't want to waste anyone's time. A person going into deliverance must have a basic understanding of the process and what is expected. If there is unwillingness to carefully follow and complete this preparation, the person should not be scheduled for a session.

Before the deliverance session, each prayee is expected to:

1. Read *Deliverance on Purpose – Power Principles that Unlock Your Destiny*.

    a. People have shared with me that my book, *Deliverance on Purpose – Power Principles that Unlock Your Destiny,* has had a profound effect in their lives. While reading, they have experienced demonic manifestation, but they have also been delivered and healed.

2. Complete our online course *Fast Lane to Freedom*.

3. Complete and send the Confidential Questionnaire (Appendix A). Do not have the person fill out the questionnaire in the manual itself, instead provide a digital copy of the Confidential Questionnaire. Honest answers and brutal transparency are vital for successful deliverance.

4. Have an interview to review the questionnaire and dig deeper into root issues.

    a. The review of the questionnaire opens your understanding and gives keen insight to the dynamic of the prayees' soul condition. With this background information, the deliverance minister will get a clear idea of the person's past sins and present tendencies and struggles that stem from them, as well as the strongholds in the prayees' life. During the interview you will be looking for demonic entry points, open doors, hurts, sinful patterns, rejection, and internal brokenness that comes from unresolved issues such as addictions, trauma, sexual sin, generational curses, etc.

    b. The interview in which we review the questionnaire with the person seeking deliverance is very important. With the help of the Holy Spirit, this is a great opportunity to discover root issues, strongholds, and demonic oppression. Asking questions shows interest and concern for the individual. The right questions will also help the person connect the dots of cause and effect – relating events in their life to subsequent oppression and other effects. The interview can be in person, via phone or Zoom.

   c. Keep in mind that the interview gives the prayee the opportunity to disclose sensitive and painful issues that have been locked up by silence for years. The prayee can receive deliverance and healing simply by telling their story.

5. Pray the prayers to renounce Free Masonry, Islam, and Catholicism.

    The prayers to renounce Free Masonry, Islam and Catholicism are found in Prayers of Release chapter. These prayers are scheduled with team members before the scheduled deliverance session.

6. Fast and pray.

7. Complete the assigned homework that consists of creating two lists.

    The forgiveness list: with the list of people who have hurt or harmed the prayee. The soul tie list: with the list of people with whom the prayee has had sexual intimacy with or without his/her consent.

    The assignment of the two lists is vital for the session. The forgiveness list touches the very depth of their being and the most sensitive issues they have ever had. Frequently we are told: "I have already forgiven everybody." But we have them forgive each person again, because in the session, there is an anointing that brings a depth of healing and true from-the-heart forgiveness. The list of names of past sexual intimacy is used in the prayers to break soul ties.

8. Prepare an offering for the deliverance ministry. An offering is important as many deliverance ministers work with little recognition. A person unwilling to invest in his / her own deliverance will most likely have a poor outcome and result of the session. Also, please remember 1 Timothy 5:18.

The above list involves a process before the Lord. Most people seeking deliverance and inner healing think the process is as quick as sprinkling holy water or waving the magic wand while sitting there passively. That is far from the truth. Everyone is different, so the time it takes to internalize and apply the information will be different for each individual. With this in mind, two weeks is considered a bare minimum to complete this initial preparation stage, though it could easily take up to two months.

Is the Prayee Sincere?

We stress the importance of personal preparation in the deliverance process. This preparation for the session is just as important as the session itself. Sincerity is essential in the quest for personal freedom. Demons can be bound and cast out, but they will in fact return if the prayee is not sincere and wants to continue in the lifestyle that caused demonic harassment and bondage. If you come to a point where the prayee is unwilling to repent, you must lovingly end the session until prayee is willing to submit that area to the Lord.

The Expected Outcome of the Preparation Phase for the Prayee

We have encountered many people that have been through other deliverance ministries. There are several things to consider here. Their previous experience could have addressed some key areas and others remained hidden; so, a new session is needed. Deep repentance and lifestyle changes perhaps never occurred after the first deliverance experience. This of course would only open the same doors to the enemy and strengthen the strongholds of the soul. Superficial repentance comes from a desire to be free from affliction but not necessarily closer to the Lord in an obedient and loving relationship.

In other words, the person wants symptomatic relief without aligning their lives with what their loving Creator desires. It is then our job to connect the two! However, remember that it is sometimes very difficult for people to open up about the most delicate and shameful areas of their life. Defense mechanisms are usually deeply entrenched; further, if they have been through other deliverance experiences, they could be fearful and mistrusting.

With those warnings in mind, we can simultaneously look forward to the good fruit of the preparation phase:

- Deep repentance.
- A desire to be truly free, whatever the cost.
- Hunger and thirst for God's will and purpose.
- Deactivation of defense mechanisms.
- Trust that God will use the team and the process.

Is it time for the Session?

To move forward with the deliverance session, we need to have several important elements in place. If the preparation is incomplete, perhaps rescheduling the session is the best alternative. Consider the following:

1. Pastoral agreement and approval of the deliverance ministry and process.

    Everything we do in ministry must be in alignment with God's authority in place over our ministry. We are accountable to God and to the local authority of the Body where He has placed us. The pastor needs to be on board with the implementation of this ministry. Also, the church must be apostolically aligned.

2. An orderly system.

    This book covers an organized structure and plan for deliverance ministry. The session itself may not follow sequentially every point, but everything outlined here needs to be addressed and considered.

3. A team in place with defined roles.

    At least 2 people must be present in the session. If serious or violent manifestations are anticipated, more is better. The team leader takes the initiative through the session. Healthy team dynamics is essential, no insecurity or animosity issues between team members. A tag team approach is good only if the level of relationship allows and under the direction of the team leader.

4. An adequate place to minister.

    Privacy is an important issue. Protect the identity of those going through the process. Since a session can last for many hours, a certain amount of comfort is important. Also, the room must be free of glass and furnishings with sharp edges or points.

5. The person scheduled for the session must prepare adequately.

    Has this person completed the above-mentioned personal preparation? Is the expected outcome of the preparation phase at an acceptable level? Always remember that personal preparation is vital for a successful outcome. Ask them to come to the session wearing pants, shirts (no low cut) and no jewelry.

Your Pre-Session Preparation as Practitioner

You need to anticipate issues before they occur. You must prepare for the session:

- Treat every day as a pre-session day. Pursue the Lord. Pray and walk in holiness. Know the fear of the Lord.
- Pray for the team: protection, wisdom, and discernment.
- Pray for the person going through deliverance.
- Pray over the questionnaire for discernment and insight that only God can provide.

Prepare water and light snacks as the session can last for hours. You have the option to plan for 2 or 3 two-hour sessions or one extended session of 4 – 6 hours.

Prayers of Release

Prayer of Release for Freemasons and their Descendants

This prayer is an important part of the deliverance process, especially for former members or descendants of Masons. The secret rituals, oaths and vows open access to the demonic realm and bring curses and infirmity. Most cities and towns across America have a lodge. Freemasonry has many representatives in law enforcement, the judicial system, and even high levels in our government. This secret organization has affected every level of our society. Pray this out loud with the deliverance practitioner or a mature Christian. Allow Holy Spirit to reveal related issues that may require further personal ministry.

> Father God, creator of heaven and earth, I come to You in the name of Jesus Christ, Your Son. I come as a sinner seeking forgiveness and cleansing from all sins committed against You. I honor my earthly father and mother and all of my ancestors of flesh and blood, and of the spirit by adoption and godparents, but I utterly turn away from and renounce all their sins. I forgive all my ancestors for the effects of their sins on me and my children. I confess and renounce all of my own sins. I renounce and rebuke Satan and every spiritual power of his affecting me and my family.
>
> I renounce and forsake all involvement in Freemasonry or any other lodge or craft by my ancestors and myself. I renounce witchcraft, the principal spirit behind Freemasonry, and I renounce Baphomet, the spirit of Anti-Christ and the curse of the Luciferian doctrine. I renounce the idolatry, blasphemy, secrecy and deception of Masonry at every level. I specifically renounce the insecurity, the love of position and power, the love of money, avarice or greed, and the pride which would have led my ancestors into Masonry. I renounce all the fear which held them in Masonry, especially the fear of death, fear of men, and fear of trusting, in Jesus' name. Amen.
>
> I renounce every position held in the lodge by any of my ancestors, including "Tyler," "Master," "Worshipful Master," or any other. I renounce the calling of any man "Master," for Jesus Christ is my only master and Lord, and He forbids anyone else having that title. I renounce the entrapping of others into Masonry, and observing the helplessness of others during the rituals. I renounce the effects of Masonry passed on to me through any female ancestor

who felt distrusted and rejected by her husband as he entered and attended any lodge and refused to tell her of his secret activities, in Jesus' name.

1st Degree: I renounce the oaths taken and curses involved in the First or entered Apprentice degree, especially their effects on the throat and tongue. I renounce the Hoodwink, the blindfold, and its effects on emotions and eyes, including all confusion, fear of the dark, fear of the light, and fear of sudden noises. I renounce the secret word, BOAZ, and all it means. I renounce the mixing and mingling of truth and error, and the blasphemy of this degree of Masonry. I renounce the noose around the neck, the fear of choking and also every spirit causing asthma, hay fever, allergies, emphysema or any other breathing difficulty. I renounce the compass point, sword or spear held against the breast, the fear of death by stabbing pain, and the fear of heart attack from this degree. In the name of Jesus Christ I now pray for healing of (the throat, vocal cords, nasal passages, sinus, bronchial tubes) and for healing of the speech area, and the release of the Word of God to me and through me, and my family in Jesus' name. Amen.

2nd Degree: I renounce the oaths taken and the curses involved in the second or Fellow Craft degree of Masonry, especially the curses on the heart, chest and lung area. I renounce the secret words JACHIN and SHIBBOLETH and all that these mean. I cut off all emotional hardness, apathy, indifference, unbelief, and deep anger from me and my family. In the name of Jesus Christ I now pray for the healing of (the chest/lung/heart area) and also for the healing of my emotions, and ask to be made sensitive to the Holy Spirit of God, in Jesus' name. Amen.

3rd Degree: I renounce the oaths taken and the curses involved in the third or Master mason degree, especially the curses on the stomach and womb area. I renounce the secret words MAHABONE, MACHABEN, MACHBINNA and TUBAL CAIN, and all that they mean. I renounce the spirit of Death from the blows to the head enacted as ritual murder, the fear of death, false martyrdom, fear of violent gang attack, assault, or rape, and the helplessness of this degree. I renounce the falling into a coffin or stretcher involved in the ritual of murder. I renounce the false resurrection of this degree, because only Jesus Christ is the Resurrection and the Life! I also renounce the blasphemous kissing of the Bible on a Witchcraft oath. I cut off all spirits of death, witchcraft and deception and in the name of Jesus Christ I now pray for healing of (the stomach, gallbladder, womb, liver, kidneys and any other organ of my body affected by Masonry), and I ask for a release of compassion and understanding for me and my family, in Jesus' name. Amen.

York Rite Degree: I renounce and forsake the oaths taken and the curses involved in the York Rite degrees of Masonry. I renounce the Mark Lodge, and the mark in the form of squares and angles which marks the person for life. I also reject the jewel or talisman which may have been made from this mark and worn at lodge meetings. I renounce the Mark Master Degree with its secret word JOPPA, and its penalty of having the right ear smote off and the curse of permanent deafness, as well as the right hand being chopped off for being an impostor, in Jesus' name. Amen.

I also renounce and forsake the oaths taken and the curses involved in the other York Rite Degrees, including Past Master, with the penalty of having my tongue split from tip to root.

I also renounce and forsake the oaths taken and the curses involved in the Most Excellent Master Degree, in which the penalty is to have my breast torn open and my heart and vital organs removed and exposed to rot on the dung hill, in Jesus' name. Amen.

Holy Royal Arch Degree: I renounce and forsake the oaths taken and the curses involved in the Holy Royal Arch Degree of Masonry, especially the oath regarding the removal of the head from the body and the exposing of the brains to the hot sun. I renounce the false secret name of God JAHBULON, and the secret password AMMI RUHAMAH and all they mean. I renounce the false communion or Eucharist taken in this degree, I renounce all the mockery, skepticism, and unbelief about the redemptive work of Jesus Christ on the cross of Calvary. I cut off all these curses and their effects on me and my family. In the name of Jesus Christ… I now pray for healing of (the brain, and the mind) in Jesus' name. Amen.

I renounce and forsake the oaths taken and the curses involved in the Royal Master Degree of the York Rite and the Select Master Degree with its penalty to have my hands chopped off to the stumps, to have my eyes plucked out from their sockets and to have my body quartered and thrown among the rubbish of the Temple. In Jesus' name. Amen.

I renounce and forsake the oaths taken and the curses involved in the Super Excellent Master Degree along with the penalty of having my thumbs cut off, my eyes put out, my body bound in fetters of brass, and conveyed captive to a strange land; and I also renounce the Knights Order of the Red Cross, along with the penalty of having my house torn down and my being hanged on the exposed timbers. In Jesus' name. Amen.

I renounce the other secret words of KEB RAIOTH and MAHER-SHALAL-HASH-BAZ and all that they mean. I renounce the vows taken on a human skull, the crossed swords, and the curse and death wish of Judas, and of having the head cut off and placed on top of a church spire. I renounce the unholy communion and especially of drinking from a human skull in this and other rites, in Jesus' name. Amen.

18th Degree: I renounce and forsake the oaths taken and the curses involved in the eighteenth degree of Masonry, and the Most Wise Sovereign Knight of the Pelican and the Eagle and Sovereign Prince Rose Croix of Heredom. I renounce and reject the Pelican witchcraft spirit, as well as the occultic influence of the Rosicrucians and the Kabbalah in this degree. I renounce the claim that the death of Jesus Christ was a "dire calamity," and also the deliberate mockery and twisting of the Christian doctrine of the Atonement. I renounce the blasphemy and rejection of the deity of Jesus Christ, and the secret words IGNE NATURA RENOVATUR INTEGRA and its meaning. I renounce the mockery of the communion taken in this degree, including a biscuit, salt and white wine. In Jesus' name. Amen.

I renounce the oaths taken and the curses involved in the American and Grand Orient Lodges, including the Secret Master Degree and its secret password ADONAI used blasphemously and its penalties;

I renounce the oaths taken and the curses involved in the Perfect Master Degree, its secret password MAH-HAH-BONE, and its penalty of being smitten to the Earth with a setting maul;

I renounce the oaths taken and the curses involved in the Intimate Secretary Degree, its secret password JEHOVAH used blasphemously, and its penalties of having my body dissected, and of having my vital organs cut into pieces and thrown to the beasts of the field;

I renounce the oaths taken and the curses involved in the Provost and Judge Degree, its secret password HIRUM-TITO-CIVI-KY, and the penalty of having my nose cut off;

I renounce the oaths taken and the curses involved in the Intendant of the Building Degree, its secret password AKAR-JAI-JAH, and the penalty of having my eyes put out, my body cut in two and exposing my bowels;

I renounce the oaths taken and the curses involved in the Elected Knights of the nine degree, its secret password NEKAM NAKAH, and its penalty of having my head cut off and stuck on the highest pole in the East;

I renounce the oaths taken and the curses involved in the Illustrious Elect of Fifteen Degree with its secret password ELIGNAM, and its penalties of having my body opened perpendicularly and horizontally, and entrails exposed to the air for eight hours so that flies may prey on them, and for my head to be cut off and placed on a high pinnacle;

I renounce the oaths taken and the curses involved in the Sublime Knights elect of the twelve Degree, its secret password STOLKIN-ADONAI, and its penalty of having my hand cut in twain;

I renounce the oaths taken and the curses involved in the Grand Master Architect Degree, and its secret password RAB-BANAIM, and its penalties;

I renounce the oaths taken and the curses involved in the Knight of the Ninth Arch of Solomon Degree, and its secret password JEHOVAH used blasphemously and its penalty of having my body given to the beasts of the forest as prey;

I renounce the oaths taken and the curses involved in the Grand Elect, Perfect and Sublime Mason Degree, its secret password, and its penalty of having my body cut open and my bowels given to vultures for food;

I renounce the oaths taken and the curses involved in the Knights of the East Degree, its secret password RAPH-O-DOM, and its penalties;

I renounce the oaths taken and the curses involved in the Prince of Jerusalem Degree, its secret password TEBET-ADAR, and its penalty of being stripped naked and having my heart pierced with a poniard;

I renounce the oaths taken and the curses involved in the Knight of the East and West Degree, its secret password ABADDON, and its penalty of incurring the severe wrath of the Almighty Creator of Heaven and Earth;

I renounce the oaths taken and the curses involved in the Council of Kadosh Grand Pontiff Degree, its secret password EMMANUEL, used blasphemously and its penalties;

I renounce the oaths taken and the curses involved in the Grand Master of Symbolic Lodges Degree, its secret password JEKSON-STOLKIN, and its penalties;

I renounce the oaths taken and the curses involved in the Noachite of Prussian Knight Degree, its secret password PELEG, and its penalties;

I renounce the oaths taken and the curses involved in the Knight of the Royal Axe Degree, its secret password NOAH-BEZALEEI-SODONIAS, and its penalties;

I renounce the oaths taken and the curses involved in the Chief of the Tabernacle Degree its secret password URIEL-JEHOVAH, and its penalty that I agree the Earth should open up and engulf me up to my neck so I perish;

I renounce the oaths taken and the curses involved in the Prince of the Tabernacle Degree, and its penalty that I should be stoned to death and my body left above ground to rot;

I renounce the oaths taken and the curses involved in the Knight of the Brazen Serpent Degree, its secret password MOSES-JOHANNES, and its penalty that I have my heart eaten by venomous serpents;

I renounce the oaths taken and the curses involved in the Prince of Mercy Degree, its secret passwords, GOMEL, JEHOVAH-JACHIN, and its penalty of condemnation and spite by the entire universe;

I renounce the oaths taken and the curses involved in the Knight Commander of the Temple Degree, its secret password SOLOMON, and its penalty of receiving the severest wrath of Almighty God inflicted upon me;

I renounce the oaths taken and the curses involved in the Grand Scottish Knight of Saint Andrew Degree, its secret password NEKAMAH-FURLAC, and its penalties;

I renounce the oaths taken and the curses involved in the Knight Commander of the Sun, or Prince Adept Degree, its secret password STIBIUM, and its penalties of having my tongue thrust through with a red-hot iron, of my eyes being plucked out, of my senses of smelling and hearing being removed, of having my hands cut off and in that condition to be left for voracious animals to devour me, or executed by lightning from heaven;

30th Degree: I renounce the oaths taken and the curses involved in the thirtieth degree of Masonry, the Grand Knight Kadosh and Knight of the Black and White Eagle. I renounce the secret passwords, STIBIUM ALKABAR, PHARASH-KOH, and all they mean. In Jesus' name. Amen.

31st Degree: I renounce the oaths taken and the curses involved in the thirty-first degree of Masonry, and the Grand Inspector Inquisitor Commander. I renounce all the gods and goddesses of Egypt, which are honored in this degree, including Anubis with the jackal's head, Osiris the Sun god, Isis the sister and wife of Osiris and also the moon goddess. I renounce the Soul of Cheres, the false symbol of immortality, the chamber of the dead and the false teaching of reincarnation and the false god RA, in Jesus' name. Amen.

32nd Degree: I renounce the oaths taken and the curses involved in the thirty-second degree of Masonry, and the Sublime Prince of the Royal Secret. I renounce the secret passwords, PHAAL/ PARASH-KOL and all they mean. I renounce Masonry's false Trinitarian deity AUM, and its parts; Brahma the creator, Vishnu the preserver and Shiva the destroyer. I renounce the deity of AHURA MAZDA, the claimed spirit and source of all light, and I renounce the worship with fire, which is an abomination to God and also the drinking from a human skull in this and other rites. I also renounce all other Hindu deities and beliefs. In Jesus' name. Amen.

33rd Degree: I renounce the oaths taken and the curses involved in the thirty-third degree of Masonry, and the Grand Sovereign Inspector General. I renounce the secret passwords, DEMOLAY, HIRUM ABIFF, FREDERICK OF PRUSSIA, MICHA, MACHA, BEALIM, and ADONAI and all they mean. I renounce all of the former obligations, including of having my tongue torn out by its roots, and all other penalties. I renounce and forsake the declaration that Lucifer is God. I renounce the cable-tow around the neck. I renounce the death wish that the wine drunk from a human skull should turn to poison and the skeleton whose cold arms are invited if the oath of this degree is violated. I renounce the three infamous assassins of the grand master, law, property and religion, and I renounce the greed and witchcraft involved in the attempt to manipulate and control the rest of mankind. In Jesus' name. Amen.

Shriners: I renounce the oaths taken and the curses involved in the Ancient Arabic Order of the Nobles of the Mystic Shrine. I renounce the piercing of the eyeballs with a three-edged blade, the flaying of the feet, the madness, and the worship of the false god Allah as the god of our fathers. I renounce the hoodwink, the mock hanging, the mock beheading, the mock drinking of the blood of the victim, the mock dog urinating on the initiate, and the offering of urine as a commemoration. In Jesus' name. Amen.

I renounce all the other oaths taken, the rituals of every degree and the curses involved. These include the Allied Degrees, The Red Cross of Constantine, the Order of the Secret Monitor, Knights of Malta, Knights Templar, the Masonic Royal Order of Scotland, Masonic Royal Order of France and Masonic Royal Order of Germany. I renounce all other lodges and secret societies such as Prince Hall Freemasonry, Mormonism, The Order of Amaranth, the Royal Order of Jesters, the Manchester Unity Order of Oddfellows, Buffalos, Druids, Foresters, Orange, Elks, Moose and Eagles Lodges, the Ku Klux Klan, The Grange, the Woodmen of the World, Riders of the Red Robe, the Knights of Pythias, the Mystic Order of the Veiled Prophets of the Enchanted Realm, the women's Orders of the Eastern Star of the Ladies Oriental Shrine, and of the White Shrine of Jerusalem, the girl's order of the Daughters of the Eastern Star, the International Orders of Job's Daughters, Rebecca's and of the Rainbow girls, and the boys' Order of De Molay, Knights of Columbus, Scientology, and any fraternities or sororities and their effects on me and all my family. In Jesus' name. Amen.

I renounce the ancient pagan teaching and symbolism of the First Tracing Board, the second Tracing board and the Third Tracing Board used in the rituals of the Blue Lodge. I renounce the pagan ritual of the "Point within a Circle" with all its bondages and phallus worship. I renounce the occultic mysticism of the black and white mosaic checkered floor with the tessellated border and five-pointed blazing star in the center. I renounce the symbol "G" and its veiled pagan symbolism and bondages. I renounce and utterly forsake the Great Architect of the Universe, who is revealed in the higher degrees as Lucifer, and his false claim to be the universal fatherhood of God. I also renounce the false claim that Lucifer is the Morning Star and Shining One and I declare that Jesus Christ is the Bright and Morning Star of Revelation 22:16. In Jesus' name. Amen.

I renounce the All-Seeing Third Eye of Freemasonry or The Egyptian God Horus and its pagan and occult symbolism. I renounce all false communions taken and all mockery of the redemptive work of Jesus Christ on the cross of Calvary. I renounce all unbelief, confusion and depression, and all worship of Lucifer as God. I renounce and forsake the lie of Freemasonry that man is not sinful, but merely imperfect, and so can redeem himself through good works. I rejoice that the Bible states that I cannot do a single thing to earn my salvation, but that I can only be saved by grace through faith in Jesus Christ and what He accomplished on the Cross of Calvary. In Jesus' name. Amen.

I renounce all fear of insanity, anguish, death wishes, suicide and death in the name of Jesus Christ. Death was conquered by Jesus Christ, and He alone holds the keys of death and hell. I rejoice that He holds my life in His hands right now. He came to give me life abundantly and eternally, and I believe His promises.

I renounce all anger, hatred, murderous thoughts, revenge, retaliation, spiritual apathy, false religions, and I renounce all unbelief, especially unbelief in the Holy Bible as God's Word, and all compromise of God's Word. I renounce all spiritual searching into false religions, and all striving to please God. I rest in the knowledge that I have found my Lord and Savior Jesus Christ, and that He has found me.

I will burn any object in my possession which connects me with all lodges and occultic organizations, including Masonry, Witchcraft and Mormonism, including all regalia, aprons, books of rituals, rings and other jewelry. I renounce the effects these or other objects of Masonry, such as the compass, the square, the noose or the blindfold, have had on me or my family. In Jesus' name. Amen.

(1) Symbolically remove the blindfold (hoodwink) and give it to the Lord for disposal;
(2) In the same way, symbolically remove the veil of mourning;
(3) Symbolically cut and remove the noose from around the neck, gather it up with the cable-tow running down the body and give it all to the Lord for His disposal;
(4) Symbolically remove the chains and bondages of Freemasonry from your body,

(5) Symbolically remove all Freemasonry regalia and armor, especially the Apron;
(6) Symbolically remove the ball and chain from the ankles;

I renounce the false Freemasonry marriage covenant, and I now remove from the 4th finger of the right hand the ring of this false marriage covenant, and I give it to the Lord.

I repent of and seek forgiveness for having walked on all unholy ground, including Freemasonry lodges and temples, including any Mormon or other occultic organizations.

Holy Spirit, I ask You to show me anything else that I need to do or to pray, so that I and my family may be totally free from the consequences of the sins of Masonry, Witchcraft, Mormonism and Paganism. In Jesus' name. Amen.

Now, Dear Father God, I ask humbly for the Blood of Jesus Christ, your Son, to cleanse me from all these sins I have confessed and renounced. To cleanse my spirit, my soul, my mind, will and emotions, and every part of my body which has been affected by these sins, in Jesus' name! Amen.

I renounce every evil spirit associated with Masonry, witchcraft, Mormonism, and all other sins, and I command in the name of Jesus Christ for Satan and every evil spirit to be bound and to leave me now, touching or harming no one, never to return to me or my family. I call on the name of the Lord Jesus Christ to be delivered of these spirits in accordance with the many promises of the Bible. I ask to be delivered of every spirit of sickness, and infirmity, and every curse, affliction, addiction, disease, or allergy associated with these sins that I have confessed and renounced. I surrender to God's Holy Spirit and to no other spirit. I ask You Lord, to baptize me in Your Holy Spirit now, according to the promises in Your Word. I take to myself the whole armor of God in accordance with Ephesians Chapter 6, and I rejoice in its protection as Jesus surrounds me and fills me with His Holy Spirit. I enthrone You, Lord Jesus, in my heart, for You are my Lord and my Savior, the source of eternal life. Thank you, Father God, for Your mercy, Your forgiveness, and Your love.

I now proclaim that Satan and his demons no longer have any legal right to mislead and manipulate me. In Jesus' name. Amen.

Acknowledgement is given to Selwyn Stevens at Jubilee Resources for providing this prayer. This is a modified version of his work. https://jubileeresources.org

Prayer of Release for Roman Catholics and their Descendants

This prayer is an important part of the deliverance process, especially for former members or descendants of Roman Catholics. Read this prayer aloud with the deliverance practitioner or a mature Christian. Allow Holy Spirit to reveal related issues that may require further personal ministry.

Father God, creator of heaven and earth, I come to you in the name of Jesus Christ your Son. I come as a sinner seeking forgiveness and cleansing from all my sins committed against you, and others made in your image. I honor my earthly father and mother and all of my ancestors of flesh and blood, and of the spirit by adoption and godparents, but I utterly turn away from and renounce all their sins. I forgive all my ancestors for the effects of their sins and iniquities on my children and me. I confess and renounce all of my own sins, known or unknown and I accept personally the sacrifice that Jesus gave Himself for me on Calvary. I renounce and rebuke Satan and every spiritual power of his affecting me and my family, in the name of Jesus Christ.

In the name of the Lord Jesus Christ, I renounce and forsake all ungodly involvement in Roman Catholicism by my ancestors and myself. I renounce every covenant, every blood covenant and every alliance with Roman Catholicism or the spiritual powers behind it made by my family or me. I also renounce and repent of all permission I have ever granted to be deceived, or that was granted by my parents or previous generations without my awareness or consent. I renounce every covenant made with death and hell.

In the name of the Lord Jesus Christ, I renounce every form of ungodly authority and all ungodly power, and I repent for submitting to all ungodly authority. I repent for my loyalty towards the Roman Catholic Church, and its Popes, Cardinals, Archbishops, Bishops and Priests when that loyalty and obedience should have been to Jesus Christ. I also repent and renounce any and all impartations I received through any laying on of hands, including by any false priesthood and all religious deception. I especially reject the false teaching and belief in the infallibility of the pope.

I repent for my silence and ignorance about the Roman Catholic Church's historical use of terror, bloodshed, torture, lies, coercion, deception, sexual immorality, fraud, control and manipulation, either directly or through the various Orders of the Church. Please heal me from any of these things that have been done to me, or that were done to others with my awareness or consent.

In the name of the Lord Jesus Christ of Nazareth, I repent for believing in a church that has kept people from understanding the Holy Bible, when that has the Words of Life. I humbly request to be exempted from the punishment for adding or deducting from God's word recorded in Revelation 22:18-19. Please help me understand Your Word the Holy Bible, and to trust it and apply it to my life in a way that will bring glory to Your name, and benefit for my spiritual growth and maturity.

In the name of the Lord Jesus Christ, I renounce the pagan syncretism taught alongside true Biblical teaching by the Roman Catholic Church. I reject and repent of all pagan beliefs and practices, and ask to be set free from all such pagan influences in my mind, my will, my emotions, my heart, my conscience, my imagination and my habits.

I choose to forgive everyone who has taught me false doctrine and ungodly religious practices, including the so-called "Sacrifice of the Mass". I also renounce and reject the calling on the spirits of the dead to protect me that occurs at every mass. In repenting for all these, I also choose to forgive myself for my active participation or acquiescent acceptance of all such beliefs and practices, in the name of Jesus Christ. I ask for mercy on all who taught me false doctrines and practices and the conviction of the Holy Spirit of the error of their ways, and that they would discover the truth and teach that instead, in Jesus' name.

In the name of the Lord Jesus Christ, I renounce and repent of every form of idolatry, including the idolatry of Holy Mother Church, and any false worship and spiritual adultery I indulged in, even in my ignorance that your Word forbids such practice in Exodus 20:5 and elsewhere. I choose to worship The True Creator God, revealed as Father, Son, and Holy Spirit. Please teach me how to worship You in spirit and in truth.

In the name of the Lord Jesus Christ, I repent and renounce every devotion, veneration, worship, and idolatry of the Virgin Mary. I also reject and renounce the falsely claimed Co-Mediatrix and Intercessory roles of Mary – the mother of Jesus – the Immaculate Conception of Mary, her Perpetual Virginity (despite having at least six other named children) and her Bodily Assumption into Heaven; all of which have no Biblical basis whatever, but are the doctrines of men imposed on Bible-deprived members.

In the name of the Lord Jesus Christ of Nazareth, I renounce the belief in the post-death apparitions of Mary, such as the Lady of Lourdes, the Lady of Fatima, the Lady of Guadeloupe, and all others. I reject all instructions from these and all other similar apparitions because too many of those instructions were contrary to the revealed Word of God. I also reject and renounce as well the other titles including the Queen of Heaven, the Lady of Mercedes, the Lady of the Snows, the Queen of Martyrs, the Queen of Peace, and Mary, Star of the Seas, the Black Madonna, and any other titles attributed to her.

In the name of the Lord Jesus Christ of Nazareth, I repent for praying to dead people and dead saints, and the necromancy and spiritism that involved, when the Holy Bible in Deuteronomy 18:11 forbids that practice.

In the name of the Lord Jesus Christ, I repent and renounce all dedication of my life to dead saints, including Mary, and also any dedication to any organization, including the Roman Catholic Church. In cancelling that now, I choose to dedicate my life to the Lord Jesus Christ, the only begotten Son of the Living God and to the purposes of His Kingdom.

In the name of the Lord Jesus Christ of Nazareth, I repent, renounce, and cut off all ungodly soul ties and connections with any dead saints that I have been dedicated to or chosen for me in my ignorance of Your Word, the Holy Bible. I repent for every time I asked any dead saint to pray on my behalf, since this practice is also forbidden in the Bible. I repent for every honor I ever performed to any dead saint where such honor was inconsistent with the Bible and God's revealed will. I ask to be set free from all confusion that praying to saints has caused, and the spiritism this involved, and I request the removal of all harmful influence they have had over my life.

In the name of the Lord Jesus Christ, I repent, and renounce all trust in dedicated objects, including medals, scapulars, statues, sacred heart posters and paintings, the rosary beads, holy water, votive candles, sacred relics, and any kissing or bowing to any alleged sacred object or novenas. I repent for trusting in religious rituals and objects as well as attributing power to them instead of trusting You Lord Jesus.

In the name of the Lord Jesus Christ, I repent and renounce all trust in any "sacrament" that does not have a solid Biblical basis, including infant baptism, confirmation, first communion or Eucharist, confession, penance, and extreme unction. I renounce all beliefs that are contrary to Your revealed Word and will including the sacrifice of Jesus celebrated during Mass. I ask for You to renew my mind and my heart, and to help me recognize all false teaching and beliefs when I hear or see them. Please protect me from all spiritual deception, regardless of source, in Jesus' name.

In the name of the Lord Jesus Christ, I reject and repent of the shameless use of indulgences to obtain money from members of the Roman Catholic Church by priests by fraud, with false and unsubstantiated promises of quicker release from the imaginary place of the dead called Purgatory, or of the falsely promised cancellation of sins.

In the name of the Lord Jesus Christ, I reject, repent, and renounce every form of sexual immorality, perversion, pedophilia, seduction, rape, the killing of babies and the hypocrisy involved in the Roman Catholic Church by priests and members of other orders over their church members and all others that has been allowed for hundreds of years. I also reject the enforced celibacy of clergy, priests, and nuns, as that is not a requirement for ministry to Jesus Christ in the Holy Bible.

Lord God, I thank you for freedom of conscience. In the name of the Lord Jesus Christ, I repent of serving a church that required people to fast through legalism, and that killed people for eating meat during Lent, and I reject the coercion of the Roman Catholic priests to live under such legalism. In the name of the Lord Jesus Christ, I repent for every instance where I tried to violate the free will of others.

Please enable me to recognize all error and false teaching. I especially renounce and repent of ever believing the anti-Biblical teachings of transubstantiation, purgatory, and that my salvation may only be obtained by being baptized into membership of the Roman Catholic Church as an infant. I recognize that the elements of communion are only symbolic of the body and blood of Jesus.

In the name of the Lord Jesus Christ, I renounce and rebuke every evil spirit associated with Roman Catholicism, spiritism, occultic mysticism and all other sins and iniquities involved. Lord Jesus, I ask you to now set me free from all spiritual and other bondages, in accordance with the many promises of the Bible. In the name of the Lord Jesus Christ, I now bind every spirit of sickness, infirmity, every curse including the curse of Trent, affliction, addiction, disease, or allergy associated with these sins I have confessed and renounced, including every spirit empowering all iniquities inherited from my family.

Holy Spirit, I ask that you show me anything else that I need to do or to pray so that my family and I may be totally free from the consequences of the sins of Roman Catholicism, Witchcraft, Spiritism and all related Paganism and Occultism.

(Pause, while listening to God, and pray as the Holy Spirit leads you.)

Now, dear Father God, I ask humbly for the blood of Jesus Christ, your Son, and my Savior, to cleanse me from all these sins I have confessed and renounced, to cleanse my spirit, my soul, my mind, my emotions and every part of my body which has been affected by these sins, in the name of Jesus Christ. I also command every cell in my body to come into divine order now, and to be healed and made whole as they were designed to by my loving Creator, including restoring all chemical imbalances and neurological functions, controlling all cancerous cells, reversing all degenerative diseases, and I sever the DNA and RNA of any mental or physical diseases or afflictions that came down through my family blood lines.

> I ask you, Lord, to fill me with your Holy Spirit now according to the promises in your Word. I take to myself the whole armor of God in accordance with Ephesians chapter six, and rejoice in its protection as Jesus surrounds me and fills me with His Holy Spirit. I enthrone you, Lord Jesus, in my heart, for you are my Lord and my Savior, the source of eternal life. Thank you, Father God, for your mercy, your forgiveness, and your love, in the name of Jesus Christ, Amen.
>
> I now command every evil spirit to leave me now, touching or harming no-one, and go to the dry place appointed for you by the Lord Jesus Christ, never to return to me or my family in the name of the Lord Jesus Christ. Amen!

Acknowledgement is given to Selwyn Stevens at Jubilee Resources for providing this prayer. This is a modified version of his work. https://jubileeresources.org

Prayer of Release from Islam

This prayer is an important part of the deliverance process, especially for former Muslims or descendants of Muslims. Read this prayer aloud with the deliverance practitioner or mature Christian. Allow Holy Spirit to reveal related issues that may require further personal ministry.

> Lord God, I confess that I have sinned and turned away from you. I repent and turn towards Christ as my Savior and Lord. Please forgive me specifically for any time when I have intimidated others, or sought to impose inferiority or humiliation on others. Forgive me for all my pride. Forgive me for any time when I have abused or dominated others. I renounce all these things in Jesus Name.
>
> Lord, I praise you for the gift of forgiveness by Christ on the cross. I acknowledge that you have accepted me. I thank you that through the cross I am reconciled to you and to others. I declare today that I am your child and an inheritor of the Kingdom of God.
>
> Father, I agree with you that I am not subject to fear, but I am a child of your love. I reject and renounce the demands of Islam as taught by Muhammad. I renounce all forms of submission to 'Allah of the Quran' and declare that I worship the God and Father of our Lord Jesus Christ and him alone.
>
> I repent for the sins of my ancestors for submitting to the *dhimma* pact and its principles, and for tithing Islam as a new nation. I ask your forgiveness for their sins, and I forgive them.

I renounce and revoke all pacts of surrender made by myself, or my ancestors to the community and principles of Islam.

I completely reject the *dhimma* and every one of its conditions. I renounce the blow on the neck in the *jizya* payment ritual, together with all that it represents. I specifically renounce the curse of decapitation and curse of death symbolized by this ritual. And I renounce all humiliation and shame. I declare that through the cross I am cleansed from all sin. Shame has no rights over me, and I will reign with Christ in glory.

I declare that the *dhimma* pact is nailed to the cross of Christ. The *dhimma* has been made a public spectacle and has no power or rights over me. I declare that the spiritual principles of the *dhimma* pact are exposed, disarmed, defeated, and disgraced through the cross of Christ.

I renounce false feelings of gratitude to Islam. I renounce false feelings of guilt or compassion. I renounce deception and lies. I renounce all agreements to keep silent about my faith in Christ.

I renounce all agreements to keep silent about the *dhimma* or Islam. I will speak and I will not be silent.

I claim the blessings of Christ as my spiritual inheritance. I renounce intimidation. I choose to be bold in Christ Jesus.

I declare that according to John 8:32 "the truth shall set me free" and I choose to live as a free person in Christ Jesus.

I renounce and cancel all curses spoken against me and my family in the name of Islam.

I renounce and cancel all curses spoken against my ancestors. I specifically renounce and break the curse of death. Death, you have no power over me! I declare that these curses have no power over me.

I renounce manipulation and control. I renounce abuse and violence. I renounce Slavery. I specifically renounce all oppression of women and children.

I renounce all fear. Fear of being rejected. Fear of losing my property and possessions. I renounce the fear of poverty. I renounce the fear of being enslaved. I renounce the fear of rape. I renounce the fear of being isolated. I renounce the fear of losing my family. I renounce the fear of being killed and the fear of death.

I renounce the fear of Islam. I renounce the fear of Muslims. I renounce the fear of being involved in public or political activity.

I declare that Jesus Christ is Lord of all. I submit to Jesus as the Lord of every area of my life. Jesus Christ is Lord of my home. Jesus Christ is Lord of my city, my state, and my nation. Jesus Christ is Lord of all peoples in this land. I submit to Jesus Christ as my Lord. I declare that Christ has accepted me. I serve Him and Him alone.

Lord, forgive me and my ancestors for all hatred toward Muslims. I renounce hatred towards Muslims and all other people and declare the love of Christ for Muslims and all other people on this earth.

I repent of the sins of the church and of wrongful submission of church leaders. I renounce alienation. I declare that I am forgiven and accepted by God through Christ. I am reconciled to God. No power in heaven or on earth can make any charge against me before the throne of God.

I declare my praise and thanks to God our Father, to Christ who is my only Savior, and to the Holy Spirit who alone gives me life. I commit myself to be a living witness to Jesus Christ as Lord and savior. I am not ashamed of His cross. I am not ashamed of His resurrection.

I declare I am a child of the living God, the God of Abraham, Isaac, and Jacob. I declare the victory of God and of His Messiah. I declare that every knee will bow, and every tongue will confess that Jesus Christ is Lord.

I declare forgiveness towards Muslims for practicing the system of dhimmitude. Father God, please free me now from the *dhimma*, the spirit of dhimmitude, and every ungodly principle attached to the *dhimma* pact.

I ask now that you fill me with your Holy Spirit, and pour upon me all the blessings of the Kingdom of Jesus Christ. Grant me grace to understand the truth of your Word clearly and to apply it in every area of my life. Grant to me words of hope and life, and bless my lips so I can speak them to others with authority and power in Jesus' name.

Give me the boldness to be a faithful witness of Christ. Grant me a deep love for Muslim people and a passion to share the love of Christ with them. I declare and ask these things in the Name of Jesus Christ my Lord and savior.

Amen.

Acknowledgment for this prayer is given to Dr. Mark Durie. Used with permission.

Dr Mark Durie is a researcher and Anglican pastor. He has published many articles and books on the language and culture of the Acehnese, Christian-Muslim relations, Islam and religious freedom. A graduate of the Australian National University and the Australian College of Theology, with a PhD in Linguistics and and ThD in Theology, he has held visiting appointments at the University of Leiden, MIT, UCLA and Stanford, and was elected a Fellow of the Australian Academy of the Humanities in 1992. mjdurie@gmail.com, https://luke4-18.com/

The Day of the Session

The big day has arrived, there is a lot of excitement and perhaps some stress or turbulence in the atmosphere. Warfare is part of the daily life of the deliverance minister. Anticipate attacks and unexpected incidents especially just before the session and immediately afterwards. The team needs to be prayed up and ready! Arrive early to set up the room, both naturally and spiritually.

The team needs to intensify their prayer in the last 24 hours before the session. That prayer should include these points:

1. Protection and safety.
2. Agreement between all team members.
3. Discernment and revelation from the Holy Spirit.
4. Greater Kingdom authority and anointing.
5. Compassion for the one seeking deliverance.
6. A heavy dose of God's love over the person seeking deliverance.

The strategy for a deliverance session is very simple. Through guided prayers of repentance and renouncing evil, we are helping the individual:

1. Close doors to demons.
2. Remove legal rights of the enemy.
3. Eject demonic intruders.

The Session Begins Here
Warm Up
Give yourself and the team a few minutes to settle into the session. Friendly small talk is good. This is a very special moment to congratulate the person seeking deliverance.

"You are a brave person to face the past and open yourself up before the Lord today."

Ask questions to clear up any doubts you might have with the questionnaire. For example:

"Is there anything you want to mention or add to what we have spoken about up to now?"

Prayer and Praise

The session starts with prayer and praise, the team together with the person scheduled for ministry. As a rule, team members always keep their eyes open for discernment and anticipating any manifestation. The team leader takes the initiative guiding through each phase of the session while team members quietly watch and pray over the person. Their role is as important as the team leader.

This prayer is a powerful way to start every session as it covers several important areas such as:

1. Affirming salvation and forgiveness of sins because of the Cross of Calvary.
2. Repentance for any sinful action, words, or thoughts.
3. Repentance for any sinful action, words or thoughts against God and parents.
4. Renouncing and breaking curses handed down through parents and prior generations.
5. Repentance and renunciation for contacts with Satan, demons, and their evil works.
6. Forgiveness to all people that have wronged or harmed.
7. Acceptance of forgiveness and the cleansing power of the blood of Jesus.
8. Calling on the Name of the Lord for deliverance and healing.

Deliverance Prayer

This prayer is used at the beginning of the first session.

Father, I humbly come before You in my time of need. I come before you because of the blood of Jesus that washes and cleanses me of all sin. I thank You Father for sending Jesus to die for me on the cross and now I can experience the depth of Your love for me.

Jesus, I thank You for dying for me and I come before You today; I accept You as my savior and confess You as the Lord of my life.

Holy Spirit I ask for clear understanding and revelation about the need and condition of my heart. I ask that You grant me deep conviction about my lifestyle and actions that displeased You as sinful behavior. Lord, I ask for Your forgiveness for every thought, action and relationship that has dishonored You. I ask for You forgiveness, cleansing and restoration by the blood of Jesus. Lord, I also ask You for a deep work of grace in my heart to overcome all forms of evil, thoughts, desires, and the inclination of my heart within as well as wickedness and darkness of this world.

I repent of and renounce all sinful thoughts, actions, and words against You Lord.
I repent of and renounce all sinful thoughts, actions and words that were against any of Your servants.
I repent of and renounce all sinful thoughts, actions and words that were against my parents that dishonored them.
I repent of and renounce all sinful thoughts, actions and words that were against any and all delegated authority over my life. I break all curses brought upon me because of these sins.

I pray Lord that You would close the doors to the enemy of my soul that I have opened because of a sinful lifestyle and remove the legal rights I have given to the enemy based on my behavior.

I repent of and renounce all forms of idolatry.
I repent of and renounce all witchcraft and occult involvement.
I repent of and renounce all contact with Satan and demons.

Lord, I ask You to cleanse me from all sin and spiritual darkness of any kind. I thank You for Your forgiveness and because of the blood of Jesus.

I am grateful for this deliverance and healing process. I thank You Lord that You open my eyes to truth and Your power will be at work to bring deep healing and powerful deliverance to my life.

I intentionally align with the Lord Jesus, the King of kings and Lord of lords. I humbly align with Your Word and Your will as a citizen of Your Kingdom here on earth. Because of the blood of Jesus, I declare that the power of darkness and demonic entities are broken in my life, and they have no place in me nor access to me. Any right demons may claim to have to remain in me, is now canceled in the name of Jesus.

I praise You Lord Jesus as my healer, deliverer, and provider. I thank You Lord for my day of deliverance and supernatural turnaround has come, this is my day of victory in the name of Jesus, amen!

Forgiveness and Inner Healing

Forgiveness

Remember the assigned homework for the session. Go through the entire list and take the time necessary to deal with everyone on the list.

Simply have the prayee:

1. Mention the name of the person being forgiven.
2. Briefly state what is being forgiven.

A simple way to do this is by saying:

> Lord, I thank You for a special grace to forgive all those who have mistreated, harmed, neglected, or abused me. Intentionally I lay aside all anger, bitterness, hatred, or resentment. I forgive _____ for _____ (what he or she did when....) and I release him / her / them in the Name of Jesus."

Frequently other names and events will come up during a session. Have the prayee forgive and release the perpetrator of the offense immediately and then continue with the process. Many times, a person seems to hold God responsible for the hurts and pain along the way. Have them forgive themselves for having this wrong impression about God. Also ask them to make a declaration releasing God and taking full responsibility for their actions. Something like "Lord, please forgive me for holding you responsible for my bad choices in life; today I understand that it was not You but me. I receive Your forgiveness."

Self-hatred and self-rejection are common reactions to making repeatedly wrong decisions through life. A powerful dynamic is self-forgiveness. The old-school hand-held mirror works best, but you can use the cell phone as well. Have the person look at him or herself and invite the prayee into self-forgiveness. They need to be specific naming the different issues in their lives. For example, "I forgive myself for having an abortion and for that adulterous relationship.

Remember that there can be several issues that result from unforgiveness. Consider the following list and pray for discernment as you minister. There is no need to address these issues during the forgiveness segment but take note and deal with them at an appropriate time in the session. However, if any of these spirits rise to resist in the forgiveness segment, you could lead the prayee in a prayer to repent of and renounce partnering with the demons. Then, go after it and cast it out.

Cancer	Hatred
Arthritis	Anxiety
Bitterness	Pride
Anger	Self-righteous
Gossip	Oppression
Revenge	Torment

Inner Healing

Just after the forgiveness prayers, is generally a perfect moment for inner healing. The act of forgiveness opens the door for the Holy Spirit to show areas in need of healing. When a person's emotions are damaged through trauma or painful experiences, a dysfunctional life is the result. The vulnerability of inner brokenness opens the door to demonic harassment and oppression.

To obtain wholeness in Christ, the wound must be healed. Inner healing repairs the damaged soul and removes the pain embedded in the memory. The result is a supernatural ability to live an empowered and renewed life in Christ. Please note that on occasion inner healing is the main element of the entire session that brings release to freedom.

In the intensity of the moment, we must resist the urge to suggest what memory or incident needs to be addressed and healed. We do not guide the person where to go into the past. We do three things in this moment:

1. We ask the Lord to bring to the prayees' mind what He wants to address and heal.

2. We lead the prayee in a prayer inviting the Holy Spirit to reveal what area He wants to deal with. (See below.)

3. We will ask the prayees' permission to proceed from this point. Sometimes the memories are extremely painful so we must be very gentle and patient.

Once a painful incident has been identified by the Holy Spirit:

1. We ask the prayee to give details about where this happened, time of day, what specific part of the house, etc. to refresh the prayee's memory and emotions.
2. We ask the prayee to look around to see if Jesus is there.
3. We ask the prayee to tell the team leader what Jesus is telling him / her and what is the expression on His face.
4. We will ask the Lord to heal the emotional pain associated with the memory.

Jesus is eternal and lives outside the realm of our chronological time frame. He was there with His beloved at that traumatic moment. When the prayee sees Jesus there, the memory is changed, and the embedded pain is removed. There is no problem if the prayee can't see Jesus. Watch facial expressions. Be careful not to confuse the release of built-up emotional pain with demonic manifestation. Allow the individual to vent the pain. It takes time and you will have to sit quietly and allow the Holy Spirit to do His work. Outbursts, screaming and crying will subside, and healing is happening right before your eyes. The healing brings immediate results. When the pain and demonic affliction is gone, uncontainable joy springs up from within. Time to smile and rejoice in the Lord!

Remember that we do not guide a person into a new replacement memory to take the place of a traumatic event. We are not asking the Lord to modify, cancel or remove the memory. This would be a New Age type practice. Also, we must be very sensitive to a person's pain. We cannot be pushy. Please keep in mind that if you are impatient or pushing through the steps, it's advisable not even to include this segment.

Prayer for Inner Healing

Lord, I come before You today knowing that my past, my present and my future is completely in Your hands. I come to You now, profoundly aware of Your presence and I intentionally open my heart to the powerful work of the Holy Spirit. I choose to submit my life to You today and always.

Lord, You know all the painful experiences that I have had over the course of my life. You are aware even of the areas that I can't see. I choose to trust You as I face the hurtful experiences of my life. I trust You with the fear, shame and rejection I have felt, knowing that You are my shield and protector.

Holy Spirit, I invite You to freely move through my heart. I give You permission to search for any trauma, hurtful memory or deep secret in my life that has affected me over the years. I know You are knocking at the door of the hidden areas of my heart. I give You permission to unlock those areas. I pray, Lord, that You will deal with any deception and any denial that has blocked Your access in the past. I also ask You, Lord, to reveal to me anything that has hindered me from my healing.

Lord, I thank you for creating true humility in my heart. I ask that You reveal to me those that I must forgive. Even though I've forgiven them in the past, I ask for an empowering grace that brings me into deep forgiveness that releases my heart from bondage and purifies my soul. By faith I forgive _____ for the hurt and turmoil that was caused by his / her actions.

Holy Spirit, I'm asking You to bring to my mind what You intend to heal today. I'm confident that You will heal me. Holy Spirit, please guide me to the right memory and, with Your loving hand, deal with the pain and heal me. My past is now in Your loving care and my present reflects that love. I thank You, Lord, for healing the brokenness, removing the pain and for my new life in Christ.

And I pray in the powerful Name of Jesus, amen!

Prayer for Healing of Parental Wounds

I forgive my father and mother for any pain they caused me, for rejection, abandonment, all abuses, for negative words toward me and any other offense, in Jesus Name!

I forgive my father and mother for all that they did to harm or hurt me in any way. I forgive my parents for all that they should have done but did not do.

I release any debt my parents have toward me as a son / daughter. I now repent of and renounce any bitter root judgement toward them, and I break the power of that judgement in the name of Jesus. I also repent and renounce the bitterness in my heart when I said, "I will never be like him / her." I pray Lord, You cleanse me of all offense, unforgiveness and a sense of self-righteousness toward my father and mother in the name of Jesus. I ask Your forgiveness for dishonoring my father and mother in my heart, with my actions or with my words. I now restore honor to my father and mother, in the Name of Jesus!

Breaking Soul Ties

A deep connection is established between two people during sexual intimacy, whether it is consensual or forced. Through that connection, two people are joined in their spirit, soul, and body. A soul tie is a term to designate the link in which demon spirits are transferred one to the another thus multiplying darkness in the two. When the relationship is severed, the soul can be fragmented or torn, and internal brokenness results.

The prayer is powerful when used with conviction and understanding. Consider the points covered:

- Submission to God.
- Repentance for illicit and ungodly relationships.
- Alignment of the inner person with God's will.
- Healing of soul fragmentation.
- Choosing to forgive others in the relationships.
- The body is offered to God as a living sacrifice.
- Breaks demonic bondages.
- Breaks demonic lies.
- Affirms inner cleansing by the blood of Jesus and self-acceptance even after impure and shameful activities.

Prayer to Break Soul Ties

Father, today I come before you to renew and strengthen my relationship with you. I recognize that I have joined my spirit, soul and body to ungodly activities that I confess and renounce, now. I ask you Lord to forgive me for all sin and involvement that has brought darkness into my life and attachments that have held me back from following you closely.

I ask you Lord to forgive me for any and all unnatural and ungodly relationships with any person, organization, place or thing. Whatever displeases you, I renounce it now. I ask you Lord to break any bondage, spiritual darkness or demonic presence that has come into my life through these relationships.

Also, I ask you to forgive me of any and all misuse of my body by sexual misconduct and intimate relations specifically with _____.

I ask you Lord that the spiritual bondage from these relationships be broken. I ask that my heart be cleansed from the attraction and remorse from these relations and that my mind would be cleansed and free from each person mentioned. I ask you Lord to free me from a false sense of responsibility for them and that you break the union and tie in the powerful Name of Jesus! I pray that the brokenness and fragmentation of my soul be healed. I say to my soul, rise up and come back together into full stature in the name of Jesus!

Today, I forgive each and every person with whom I have had an ungodly relationship. I also choose to forgive myself for involvement in these relationships. I choose to no longer punish myself or be angry with myself for this involvement. Furthermore, I offer my life to you Lord as a living sacrifice. I place myself on the altar as a love offering knowing that my life is seen as holy and acceptable.

I thank you Lord today that I am cleansed, spirit, soul and body. I know now that I am forgiven and your love for me is eternal and unconditional. I now align my whole spirit, soul and body with the Father's Kingdom purposes and I offer my life to fulfill them by working to build your influence in the earth!

I thank you for this powerful encounter with your love in the Name of Jesus, amen!

At the end of this prayer, we sometimes do a prophetic act of symbolically severing all cords, ties, and attachments off the back of the person. Also, we confront and break any demonic entity attached to the individual based on this prayer.

Now, the person will take both lists (forgiveness and soul ties) and tear them up into little pieces.

Encourage the prayee to stomp on the pieces and jump up and down on them because the power of unforgiveness and soul ties have been broken in the Name of Jesus! Additionally, we get on the floor with the prayee to pick up the pieces of paper. This is done as a prophetic act, symbolically, to help the prayee take out the trash!

Terminating Generational Curses

Unrepented sin of our ancestors becomes the power of iniquity of subsequent generations. This tendency to sin in specific areas in patterns and cycles is known as a generational curse.

Every individual is led through a series of prayers to repent of all personal involvement in the sins of the fathers. The prayers also include renouncing and breaking those curses in the Name of Jesus.

We see these three areas throughout the deliverance process and especially in the generational curse segment:

1. Repentance of sin
2. Renouncing sinful activity
3. Breaking curses
4. Replace the iniquitous structure with a biblical truth.

Poverty and Ignorance

Robbing God	Boredom	Prostitution
Stealing	Apathy	Drug dealing
Gambling	Entitlement	Bankruptcy
Lack	Fear of the future	Business failure
Wasteful spending	Temporal satisfaction	Debt
Cycles of misery	Rejecting God's ways	Rejects education
Pride	Shame	Dishonesty
Depression	Blame shifting	Destitution
Rebellion	Injustice	Spiritual poverty
Procrastination	Inability to produce	Laziness
Bondage	Unworthiness	Unbelief

Abandonment

Rejection of others	Loneliness	Separation
Self-rejection	Self-pity	Divorce
Perceived rejection	Emptiness	Emotional pain
Rejecting God	Neglect	Desertion

Mental Torment

Fear (all kinds)	Terror	Hopelessness
Phobias	Hearing Voices	Insomnia
Dread	Intimidation	Fantasies
Worry	Heaviness	Dissociation
Paranoia	Depression	Hallucinations
Insanity	Discouragement	Confusion
Death wish	Gloom	Nervousness
Schizophrenia	Despair	Weariness
Anxiety	Affliction	Emotionally unstable
Emotional pain	Doublemindedness	Harassment
Mental Illness	Madness	Hysteria

Rejection

Rejection of self	Shame	Self-mutilation
Rejection of God	Failure	Self-hatred
Perceived Rejection	Anger	Depression
Anticipated Rejection	Eating disorders	Suicide
Rejecting love	Rejecting help	Rejecting friendship

Anger and Violence

Malevolence	Contentious	Frenzy
Quarrelsome	Hotheaded	Brutality
Outbursts	Embittered	Aggressive
Rage	Vengeful	Overpowering

Enrage
Outrage
Angriness
Fury
Punishment

Retaliation
Premature death
Cruelty
Abuse
Arguing

Temper
Murder
Torture
Harm
Cursing

Rebellion
Undermine
Overthrow
Treachery
Treason
Self-willed
Control

Defiance
Disobedience
Dishonor
Insubordination
Defiance
Witchcraft

Resist authority
Sabotage
Subversion
Contempt
Secretive
Idolatry

Manipulation
Control
Deception
Mind control
Guilt trip
Flattery

Dominate
Passive aggressive
Belittle
Sarcasm & contempt
Withhold / divulge info

Occult control
Witchcraft
Jezebel / Ahab
Emotional abuse

Religion and Cults
Control & Power
Deception
Religious spirit
Manipulation
Legalism
Ritual

Tradition
Religious pride
New Age
Progressive & Liberal
False righteousness
Inquisition

Excommunication
Division
Antichrist
Extortion
Coerced submission
Idolatry

Pride
Superiority
Haughtiness

Self-centeredness
Cockiness

Narcissism
Conceit

Arrogance
Boastfulness
Ridicule
Manipulative

Egotism
Big headed
Loftiness
Sarcastic

Leviathan
Mockery
Snobbish
Self-exaltation

Sickness

Illness
Vulnerable
Emotional pain
Affliction
Undiagnosed disease
Infections
Lingering weakness

Cancer
Diabetes
Mental illness
Migraines
Feebleness
Disfunction
Hypochondria

Eyes
Lungs
Heart
Digestive
Bi-polar
Obesity
Many others

Addictions

Illegal drugs
Legal Rx
Alcohol
Cigarettes
Escape
Tranquilizers
Shopping
Music

Social media
Pornography
Sex
Food
Sports
Television
Hoarding
Fantasy world

Affirmation
Slumber
Withdrawal
Passivity
Video games
Gambling
Emotional pain
Emptiness

Sexual Sin and Perversion

Fornication
Adultery
Incest
Incubus
Succubus
Masturbation
Sexual fantasies
Sexual slavery

Prostitution
Gender dysphoria
Homosexuality
Lesbianism
Pansexuality
Idolatry
Bestiality
Sex toys

Anal / oral sex
Seduction
Sadomasochism
Voyeurism
Sexual abuse
Rape
Frigidity
Depravity

Witchcraft and Occult

Fetish and charms	Black / white magic	Martial arts
Enchantments	Voodoo	Horoscopes
Magic potions	Santería	Idolatry
Incantations	Wicca	Animal sacrifices
Amulet	Conjuring spirits	Ouija board
Crystal gazing	Necromancy	Mental Telepathy
Fortune telling	Exorcism	Abortion
Astral projection	Hexes and spells	Death
Divination	Eastern meditation	Suicide
Palm reading	Channeling demons	Many more

Internal Brokenness

Dysfunction	Despair	Anguish
Heartbreak	Emotional pain	Bullying
Torment	Grief	Depression
Abuse (all kinds)	Entrapment	Passivity
Trauma	Torment	Suspicion
Loss	Helplessness	Victim
Codependency	Guilt & Shame	Unworthiness

Prayer of Release from Generational Curses

Father, I want to thank You, for I understand that Your intention is to bring blessings upon my life, my family, and my children. I thank You Lord Jesus for Your death on the cross to redeem me from all curses /ancestral iniquity, and to free me from all transgressions and rebellion. Lord Jesus, I come before You in praise and thanksgiving, and with the full intent of taking hold of all the blessing and freedom that are now legally paid for! Jesus, You became a curse for me so I can be fully redeemed from all curses! Thank You Lord!

Your Word has been revealed and I see the spiritual inheritance that has come to me through my ancestors. Holy Spirit, I ask You to reveal to me the cause of the curses in my life. Today, I come before You Lord to begin the process of renouncing and repenting for the iniquity of my ancestors.

I ask You Lord for the forgiveness of each and every sin of my ancestors that have contributed to the generational curses in my life. Today I specifically confess the sins of my ancestors.

(Mention the specific sins now from the above listing and others that the Holy Spirit brings to mind.)

I renounce their sin and rebellion and I ask You to forgive me for my participation in their sins. I thank You Lord that You forgive me now. I thank You for releasing me from all the curses! With the authority given me in Christ, I break the power of these curses that have come over my life in the name of Jesus.

I declare that by the blood of Jesus, generational curses are broken. I cancel the assignment of the enemy to destroy my life through those curses. I break all power of the enemy coming against me and I cancel all assignments against my life and family in the name of Jesus. By my repentance and renouncing the lifestyle of my ancestors I declare that my children are blessed and sheltered from all generational curses.

I declare that familiar spirits have no legal right or access to my life based on the sins of my ancestors. I come against every demon that has attached itself to my DNA and entered through my bloodline. I cast it away from me now and I break its power in my life in the Name of Jesus! I thank You Lord that I am free from generational curses and free to enter into a life of the fulfillment of Your love and the fullness of Your blessings for me according to Your written Word. In the Name of Jesus, amen!

Revoking Agreement with Darkness

Agreement with darkness occurs when an ungodly belief is embraced and acted upon as truth. An ungodly belief is a demonic lie and therefore contrary to the Word of God. When a parent scolds a child as being stupid over and over, an ungodly belief is formed. Unfortunately, this lie of the enemy becomes the realty later in life. Ungodly beliefs are very destructive and must be identified, renounced, broken, and then replaced by the Word of God.

This segment doesn't necessarily have chronological order. The ungodly beliefs can come to light at any phase of the deliverance and healing process. If the lie is foundational in the person's life, it is wise to take a moment to address the ungodly belief as soon as it has been detected.

Why a person came to believe a lie can be helpful but not of major consequence. The why usually points to an individual or incident. Much of modern counselling revolves around discovering the "why" of the client's problems. Keep in mind that discovering the "why" may result in blame shifting. It's much more important to discover what the ungodly beliefs are with the end of taking responsibility for them and replace them with godly and biblical beliefs that bring renewal of the mind and lifestyle transformation.

An ungodly belief, when embraced and accepted, sooner or later is expressed with words. When the lie is spoken, it then activates oppressive demonic activity. Therefore, prayers to repent and break the lies of the enemy are crucial to walk in freedom.

Sources of the Enemy's Lies

- Culture.
- Friends and family.
- Musical lyrics.
- Popular television programs and movies.

- Words curses from people.
- Literature, philosophy, and the government school system
- Social media.

Here's a step-by-step process that you can apply to your life. And, as a deliverance minister, lead others in this process:

- Identify the lie.
- Identify where the lie came from.
- Forgive the people involved in forming the lie.
- Write down the truth from the Word.
- Embrace the truth from God's Word to replace the lie.
- Apply the truth in a practical way until it becomes a part of your lifestyle.

Prayer to Break Demonic Lies

Father, I come before the truth of Your Word and the truth personified in the Lord Jesus. I pray that the Holy Spirit will create in me a passionate desire to know Your Word. Holy Spirit, I ask You to reveal to me any and all agreements I have with darkness. I ask You, Lord, to reveal any and all lies that entered during my childhood and in any traumatic moment of my life. I open my heart to You Lord, knowing that You are my savior and deliverer. I forgive all those who contributed towards the formation of the lies I have believed.

I recognize I have believed the lie that says: _____.

I repent of all sins associated with that lie.

I renounce a lifestyle that perpetuates the darkness of that lie.

I break the power of that lie over me and my descendants in the name of Jesus!

I replace the lie with the truth from Your Word that says: _____.

Your Word says in Ephesians 3:20 that You do everything exceedingly abundantly more than I can ask or think. I thank You for Your Word. I dare to believe You for light, truth, freedom, and the fulfillment of everything You have called me to do and to be in the Name of Jesus.

I am determined and resolute in my desire to embrace and apply Your Truth to every area of my life: spirit, soul, and body, as well as my past, present and future. I thank You for the healing power of Your presence that enters my life right now, and for the infilling of Your Spirit. In the Name of Jesus, amen!

Demolishing Strongholds

By this time the prayee has been prepared adequately; you have also dealt with several big issues of deliverance and inner healing. The process up to this point is designed to remove legal rights of the enemy by prayers of repentance and renunciation. Demons no longer have a tight grip on the prayee. Inner healing has brought wholeness to the soul and the vulnerability to demonic harassment has been significantly reduced. This is the section to confront demons and cast them out, once and for all. By doing so, the open doors to the enemy will be closed and strongholds destroyed.

Keep in mind that strongholds are formed by:

- The family, cultural values, and traditions.
- Personal interests and study of areas incompatible to the Word of God.
- Generational iniquity.
- Personal sin.
- Trauma and the hurts of the past.
- Soul ties.

Strongholds are formed through the collective impact of darkness embedded in the soul throughout a person's lifetime. The cumulative effect of darkness and destruction from the enemy over the years form an internal structure in a person's mind and emotions. That structure determines lifestyle, moral choices, and religious and philosophical convictions. Outlook on life and behavioral patterns are all processed in a way that is consistent with the stronghold. Furthermore, since these strongholds are deep within the soul, they go without detection for years because they are so well protected by a system of lies, half-truths, lusts of the flesh, as well as cultural influences.

Lead the prayee in a simple prayer to renounce any manifestation and all fruit of each applicable stronghold. The prayer is brief, here is an example with the Stronghold of Fear:

I repent of partnering with fear and I renounce the Stronghold of Fear with all its fruit and manifestations. I also renounce the familiar spirits of fear in the name of Jesus. And I break all spirits of fear over my life and the life of my descendants in the Name of Jesus. Amen!

Then, go after it. Cast out demons!

The Stronghold of Antichrist
Attitudes and Mindsets

- Spiritual, religious, and ideological pride.
- Against anything Jewish or Christian. Supports BDS.
- Does not need "more" of Jesus and seeks no fresh encounter with Holy Spirit.
- Easily mixes the Holy and the profane.
- Ideologies such as Nazism, Socialism, Communism, and Islam.
- Sees no evil in the liberal progressive "woke" agenda.
- Wholehearted support for the LGBTQ+ agenda
- False religions such as Mormonism, Catholicism, Freemasonry, New Age, Cults, and secular humanism.

Expressions and Manifestation

- Aligns with corporations and government agencies that mandate antichristian values.
- Jesus is reduced to the status of a prophet or teacher like many others.
- Vocal opposition to the gifts of the Holy Spirit.
- Resists the conviction of the Holy Spirit.
- Denies the divine inspiration for the Bible, the deity of Christ and the need for atonement by Jesus' death on the cross.
- Loves ungodly music, entertainment, and has little or no desire for personal holiness.
- Mockery or persecution of the truth.

Spirits Associated with the Stronghold of Antichrist

Lawlessness	Deception	New Age
Rebellion	Accusation	Kundalini
Religious spirit	Python or serpent	Spirit of Religion
Idolatrous spirit	Mermaid	Lying spirit
Ahab or Jezebel	Marine spirits	Blasphemy
Spirit of Blindness	Corruption	Obscenities

The Stronghold of Anger and Jealousy
Attitudes and Mindsets

- Frustration for feeling left out and mistreated.
- Coveting the success, wealth, possessions, and prominence of others.
- Anger and rage against the wealthy and powerful.
- Extreme desire to win in all competition.
- Vengeance, violent revenge and even murder for major offense.
- Hatred, racism, and bigotry against "undesirable" people groups.
- Contention, strife, and divisiveness in key relationships.
- Suspicion and passive aggression.
- Cruelty and spite.
- Selfishness and self-centeredness are foundational.
- Justification of personal sin.
- Capitalism is evil. Socialism is the way.
- Systemic racism and historical injustice require reparations.

Expressions and Manifestation

- I am always right despite the facts.
- My anger is justified by the offense.
- The jealousy is so strong that I lose control and become violent.
- I feel justified in my anger.

Spirits Associated with the Stronghold of Anger and Jealousy

Jealousy	Anger	Frustration
Hatred	Rage	Pride
Revenge	Murder	Strife
Resentment	Racism	Selfishness
Envy	Division	Covetousness
Argumentative	Cruelty	Suspicion

The Stronghold of Bondage
Attitudes and Mindsets
- I can't control my actions.
- I enjoy this too much; it's much to give up. I don't think this is too bad.
- I am stuck and can't break out of this.
- I am so tired of trying to hide this addiction.
- I am so dissatisfied and depressed all I can do is get high again.
- This is a vicious cycle. I am a useless individual.
- It's too late, I've lost everything.
- This _____ makes me happy.
- Hopelessness and failure are core mindsets.
- Fantasy and escape are more important than life itself.
- My feelings are at the center of everything.
- I have never been happy, but I deserve to be happy and feel good.

Expressions and Manifestation
- Fear of man, death, and the truth about my shameful life.
- Addictions: drugs and alcohol, sex, pornography, masturbation, cigarettes, food, gaming, shopping, gambling.
- Compulsive behavior and sin.
- Religious bondage: tradition, idolatry, and ancestor worship.
- Bitterness and unforgiveness because of injustice or trauma.
- Inability or unwillingness to break out of the addiction cycle.
- Failure to comprehend the magnitude of the sin and consequences.

Spirits Associated with the Stronghold of Bondage

Fear	Addiction	Destruction
Shame	Lust	Religious Tradition
Hopelessness	Perversion	Idolatry
Death	Insecurity	Captivity
Suicide	Bondage	Blindness
Bitterness	Unforgiveness	Escape

The Stronghold of Deaf and Dumb
Attitudes and Mindsets
- Feels pushed to self-destructive behavior and suicide.
- Self-hatred, self-mutilation, and self-punishment.
- Pining away: a life progressively diminished because of loss or sadness.

Expressions and Manifestations
- Tendency to do dumb things but can be very intelligent.
- Physical and spiritual blindness, deafness, and dumbness.
- Mental problems and paranoia.
- Sudden falling to the ground, foaming at the mouth and gnashing teeth.
- Convulsion, stupor, or catatonic states.
- Detachment from reality and relationships.
- Spiritual slumber and dullness. Inability to connect with God and hear His voice.
- Difficulty to speak and communicate effectively and accurately.

Spirits Associated with the Stronghold of Deaf and Dumb

Slumber	Mental Illness	Dissociation
Deaf	Self-destruction	Detachment
Dumb	Self-hatred	Seizures
Mute	Suicide	Death
Stupor	Confusion	Insanity

The Stronghold of Death and Destruction
Attitudes and Mindsets

- I want it even if it kills me. Flirting with death is exciting.
- I am in a hopeless descent into darkness.
- There is a twisted sense of pleasure in my ruined life.
- Everything I do seems to fall apart. Important relationships always fall apart.
- Pleasure is the way to go in this world full of pain and suffering.
- Intentional destructive behavior with no regard to consequences.
- Fatalism and pessimism are the lifestyle.
- Passivity and resignation facing difficult life circumstances.

Expressions and Manifestations

- Recklessness, clumsiness, and accidents. Dare devil acts.
- Rash and irresponsible lifestyle. Distraction, deception and resulting destruction.
- Unusually prone to life threatening disease.
- Attitudes and actions that undermine and destroy key relationships and ministry opportunities.
- Miscarriages and abortion.
- Aggressive and belligerent behavior.
- Robbery and financial ruin.
- Divorce and dissociation from reality.

Spirits Associated with the Stronghold of Death and Destruction

Self-destruction	Death	Murder
Self-hatred	Grief	Hatred
Suicide	Hostility	Hopelessness
Depression	Disease	Violence
Divorce	Destruction	Reckless

In dealing with this stronghold, we must break the assignment of death and destruction to marriage and family, key relationships, calling, anointing, financial position, and dreams of a better future.

The Stronghold of Error
Attitudes and Mindsets
- A divisive, argumentative, and defensive attitude.
- Wants to correct the world but doesn't allow correction.
- Teaches others while being unteachable.
- Considers most spiritual leaders as false.
- Hyper spirituality and unsubmissive heart.
- Desires to manifest spiritual gifts for personal advantage and validation.
- Godless ideologies such as: Socialism, Communism, Nazism, DEI, CRT, etc.
- Promotes the teachings of false doctrines such as: Freemasonry, Islam, Catholicism, Mormonism, Jehovah's Witnesses, Hinduism, Buddhism, New Age, Witchcraft, Antisemitism, Cessationism, etc.
- On a personal mission to show the Church the "correct path."
- An overwhelming desire to operate in the supernatural realm.

Expressions and Manifestations
- Twists clear Bible truths to fit in to false doctrine.
- Serious difficulty with seeking God in prayer, and Bible study.
- Hindrance in church involvement, understanding preaching and flowing in the Holy Spirit.
- Demonic harassment, affliction, and physical pain. Mental confusion and fear.
- A form of godliness and an ungodly lifestyle.
- Mixes the holy and the profane.
- Religious showmanship and false messiahs.

Spirits Associated with the Stronghold of Error

Deception	Hypocrisy	Legalism
Self-deception	Seduction	Confusion
Pride	Blindness	Error
Antichrist	Perversion	Self-promotion
Rebellion	Divination	Contention

The Stronghold of Fear
Attitudes and Mindsets

- Trigger moments based on past traumatic events.
- Irrational pleasure in watching terror and horror movies.
- Attraction based on biochemical and emotional high.
- Pain or loss is in my path.
- Irrational panic or anxiety of what might exist out there.
- Conscious and unconscious existence of and predisposition for fear.
- Imagined threats are real.

Expressions and Manifestations

- Disproportionate and unreasonable fear of what could happen.
- Situational fear such as: public speaking, heights, elevators, flying etc.
- Phobias such as:
    - Animals – snakes, dogs, spiders, bugs, bats
    - Nature and Weather – storms, hurricanes, tornadoes, fires
    - Medical procedures – blood, dentists, injections, pain
    - Tight and enclosed spaces
- Social anxiety and fear in personal relationships: embarrassment, shame, guilt, jealousy, etc.
- Fear of authority, abuse, men, women, rejection, abandonment, failure, future, lack, conflict, not measuring up to a standard, death, many more…
- Distorted image of God that produces fear.
- Emotional paralysis and oppression.

Spirits Associated with the Stronghold of Fear

Fear	Torment	Abandonment
Anxiety	Horror	Distrust
Worry	Recluse	Phobias
Dread	Unbelief	Panic
Hermit	Death	Darkness

The Stronghold of Heaviness and Rejection
Attitudes and Mindsets

- Loneliness is better than faking happiness.
- Indifference and lack of motivation.
- Feels unworthy of love and never good enough.
- There is no value in life, and I am unwanted.
- No one would really miss me when I'm gone.
- Feels that there may be no moral absolutes or truth.

Expressions and Manifestations

- Emotional instability, low self-esteem, and pessimism.
- Inability to receive love.
- Antisocial behavior and withdrawal.
- Difficulty in focusing on the task at hand.
- Emotional and spiritual paralysis.
- Broken heart, abandonment, and fatherlessness.
- Rejection, fear of rejection, perceived rejection, anticipated rejection.
- Exhaustion and tired of the disillusionment of life.
- Deep regret for personal failures.
- Thinks frequently about death.
- Eating disorders: gluttony, bulimia, and anorexia.

Spirits Associated with the Stronghold of Heaviness and Rejection

Abandonment	Grief	Emotional pain
Heaviness	Mourning	Darkness
Depression	Despair	Dejection
Rejection	Self-pity	Gloom
Sorrow	Self-hatred	Death
Shame	Broken heart	Suicide
Lying	Emptiness	Self-mutilation

The Stronghold of Infirmity
Attitudes and Mindsets

- Embraces unhealthy lifestyle, eating habits and self-curses.
- The disease is inevitable. "If it's out there, I get it."
- Powerless and defeatist mentality.
- Constant complains of bodily discomfort.
- Favorite theme for discussion.
- Emotional satisfaction and attention for being sick.
- Conforms to medical diagnosis and takes ownership of the disease.
- Believes that a contagious illness will always hit personally and at home.
- Views life through the lens of disease.

Expressions and Manifestations

- Frequently references to physical weaknesses and "my diseases".
- Fear of illness.
- Generational iniquity that produces disease.
- Infirmity: weakness and frailness spirit, soul, and body.
- Emotional and spiritual paralyses.
- Crippling of the body, soul, and spirit.
- Death wish.

Door openers to spirits of infirmity:

Moral and spiritual weakness, the occult, pagan and witchcraft practice, idolatry, trauma, depression, unforgiveness, bitterness, poor hygiene, gluttony.

Spirits Associated with the Stronghold of Infirmity

Death	Suffering	Depression
Trauma	Sorrow	Witchcraft
Timidity	Paralysis	Affliction
Fear	Abuse	Torment

The Stronghold of Lying
Attitudes and Mindsets
- Enjoys legalism, self-promotion and promoting personal agenda.
- Relishes the ability to control and manipulate people.
- Loves spiritual manifestations with no desire for discernment.
- Tends to easily succumb to demonic lies and bows under criticism of others.
- Religious feelings that promote guilt, shame, and condemnation.
- Lies and then believes the lies as truth.
- Antichristian ideologies.
- Prefers to see the glass half full and a negative outlook on life.
- Thrives with a sense of power from manipulation and giving false prophecies.
- Personal beliefs as truth are equal in value or better than beliefs of others.

Expressions and Manifestations
- Embraces lies unknowingly. False Memories.
- New Age and occult involvement rejecting biblical revelation.
- Aligns with the kingdom of darkness and rejects Holy Spirit instruction.
- Ignorance of biblical truth.
- Follows and or promotes false teachers and false prophecy.
- Believes in good / bad luck, superstition, and old wives' tales.
- Easily manipulated.
- Exaggeration, gossip, and flattery.
- Gender identity confusion, gay / lesbian, transgender movement.

Spirits Associated with the Stronghold of Lying

Lying	Exaggeration	Guilt
Error	Flattery	Shame
Deception	Slander	Condemnation
Self-deception	Accusation	Compromise
Legalism	Unbelief	Darkness
Slumber	Division	Superstition

The Stronghold of Poverty
Attitudes and Mindsets
- Shame and embarrassment.
- Inferiority, low self-esteem, and fatherlessness.
- Doesn't care about the long-term effect of the lifestyle.
- Seeks peer approval over wise decisions.
- Rejects opportunities for self-improvement and financial progress.
- Foolishness in decision making and conforms to circumstances.
- Lifestyle of temporal satisfaction fed by internal pain.
- Prefers temporal pleasure over hard work that opens a better future.
- Conscious rejection of God's wisdom and plan for the abundant life.
- Embraces socialism and communism. Entitlement mentality.
- Unwilling to give tithes and offerings. Lack of generosity.

Expressions and Manifestations
- Generational curse of poverty and ignorance.
- Depression and hopelessness.
- Inability and lack of desire for personal advancement.
- Seemingly endless cycles of personal and family misery and destitution.
- Preference to embrace the lies of the enemy instead of acting upon opportunities for personal advancement.
- Rejection, abuse, abandonment, and fatherlessness.
- Spiritual and intellectual blindness.
- Fear of lack and inability to overcome life's challenges.

Spirits Associated with the Stronghold of Poverty

Anger	Apathy	Bondage
Jealousy	Pain	Addiction
Laziness	Trauma	Shame
Boredom	Fear	Blindness
Rejection	Lying	Depression
Poverty	Ignorance	Misery

The Stronghold of Religion
Attitudes and Mindsets
- Enjoys projecting the appearance of spirituality.
- Creates a self-styled spirituality and religion.
- Trusts in church hierarchy and doctrine over scriptural principles.
- Craving for honor and personal recognition in church.
- Internal pressure to perform.
- Extreme passion to correct spiritual "error" in others.
- Establishes nonbiblical beliefs and customs as truth.
- A form of "godliness" but denies God's power in action. Holier than thou.
- Tradition is of greater value than Biblical truth.
- Liturgical and ritual expressions over the work of Holy Spirit.
- All religions lead to the same higher consciousness otherwise known as heaven.

Expressions and Manifestations
- Mechanical and repetitive religious prayer, going through the motions.
- Spiritual slumber that allows manipulation and control.
- Occult, new age and syncretism.
- Seduces and deceives through spiritual error.
- Counterfeit spiritual manifestations and gifts.
- Attempts to imitate the work of the Holy Spirit.
- Harsh judgmental attitude and imposes personal lack of peace and joy on others.
- False righteousness and holiness.
- Rigid and unyielding, refusal of change.

Spirits Associated with the Stronghold of Religion

Poverty	Accusation	Deception
Bitterness	Confusion	Seduction
Pride	Shame	Hypocritical
Anger	Guilt	Manipulation
Persecution	Lying	Control
Judgement	Rebellion	Self-righteous

The Stronghold of Seduction
Attitudes and Mindsets

- Sees the blind spots in people and takes advantage of them to manipulate.
- Attracts and allures with the promise of pleasure or reward.
- Persistent charm with an appeal to the senses.
- Pressure to violate the conscience and breaks down the will and personal convictions. Isolates to control.
- Appeals to the senses to attract and if it doesn't get its way turns against.
- Plays on the weakness of others to overcome and exercise power over.
- Progressive and systematic attack to break down the structures and convictions.
- Heightened sense of self-importance and preeminence.

Expressions and Manifestations

- Uses apparent insecurity and false humility to exploit.
- Uses flattery and soft speech to charm and set up the victim.
- Sexual, religious, doctrinal, political.
- Entices disobedience and covenant breaking.
- Uses pressure and manipulation to obtain the desired end.

Spirits Associated with the Stronghold of Seduction

Predator	Charm	Baiting
Victim	Flattery	Enticing
Attraction	Confusion	Manipulation
Allure	Entrapment	Control

The Stronghold of Perversion
Attitudes and Mindsets

- Turns away from what is right and pure. Leaves the first love.
- Loves to have power, control, and domination, especially sexually.
- Narcissistic self-gratification plays a major role in life.
- Love of money.
- Twists the Word of God and embraces moral decline.
- Morbid interest in pornography, sexual fantasies, exposure, voyeurism.

Expressions and Manifestations

- Spiritual whoredom, adultery, unfaithfulness, and sexual slavery.
- Chasing after self-pleasing, flesh pleasing activities.
- Adultery of the spirit, soul, and body.
- Undermines love and devotion to the Lord.
- Persistent dissatisfaction, lust, and excessive appetites.
- Rape, incest, child abuse and molestation.
- Effeminate men and masculine women.
- Satanic Ritual Abuse, satanic dedications and wedding ceremonies, Incubus, Succubus, Lilith.

Spirits Associated with the Stronghold of Perversion

Perversion	Prostitution	Unclean
Idolatry	Incubus	Whoredom
Adultery	Succubus	Lust
Fornication	Lilith	Brokenness

Sexual perversions are spirits:

Rape, prostitution, orgies, oral, anal, masturbation, incest, homosexual, lesbian, bisexual, polyamory, sadomasochism, bestiality, others.

Cast out the relevant sexual perversion spirits mentioned above by name when needed. Example:

> "Come out spirit of masturbation in the name of Jesus."

The Stronghold of Pride and Arrogance
Attitudes and Mindsets
- Complaining and lack of gratitude.
- Inflated self-importance and perfectionism.
- Resists acknowledging wrong and asking for forgiveness.
- Blame shifting, defensiveness, sarcastic and talks down to others.
- Minimizes personal sin and overemphasizes sin of others.
- Impatient, disrespectful, and irritable dealing with people.
- Unteachable spirit, resists authority and self-righteous.
- Manipulating and using people for selfish ends.
- Selfish self-centered lifestyle with elitist superiority.
- Deserves acceptance, special recognition, status, and position ahead of others.
- Always right and going to great lengths to prove it.

Expressions and Manifestations
- My / our _____ is better than yours!
- Flaunting physical beauty or sexuality.
- Personal, professional, sexual, cultural, national, religious pride
- Pushy, overbearing, and dominant.
- False humility, narcissism, and self-promotion.
- Control and manipulation.
- Seeks attention and the spotlight.
- Deceptive, deceitful and covers sins.
- Rejects authority (God's, Kingdom delegated and civil).
- Cycles of falling into sin, broken relationships, financial ruin, and addictions.

Spirits Associated with the Stronghold of Pride and Arrogance

Pride	Mockery	Vain
Arrogance	Narcissist	Critical
Manipulation	Leviathan	Haughty
Control	Superiority	Contentious
Rebellion	Self-righteous	Selfish
Division	Obstinate	Scornful
Stubborn	Strife	Dissention

The Stronghold of Witchcraft and Divination
Attitudes and Mindsets
- Fascination with darkness and evil.
- Lust for power, control and to uncover hidden knowledge occult practices.
- Enjoys passive mind states, New Age visualization and meditation.
- Loves Harry Potter, demonic movies, music, games, and books.
- Rebellion against the Judeo-Christian biblical heritage.

Expressions and Manifestations
- Drug use: hallucinogens and psychedelic to connect with the spirit world.
- Spiritual mind control and slumber.
- Afro-Caribbean witchcraft, Voodoo, Santería, and Catholic syncretism.
- Spirit and animal guides and imaginary friends.
- Necromancy, divination, fortune teller, soothsayer, psychics, false prophecy.
- Use of charms, magic for protection, love, and good luck.
- European witchcraft, Paganism, Wicca, all magic, Druid and Celtic witchcraft.
- Shamanism, witchdoctors, and shapeshifting.

There are many practices associated with witchcraft and divination:

Satanism, stargazer, zodiac, horoscopes, astrology, birth charts, witch, warlock, sorcerer, wizard, hypnotist, enchanter, automatic handwriting and analysis, astral projection, water witching, Freemasonry, spiritism, mediums, séances, numerology, reflexology, superstition, martial arts, acupuncture, yoga, channeling, remote viewing, mantras, chanting, talismans, symbols, hand seals, mudras, 3rd Eye, clairvoyance, clairaudience, telepathy, tea leaves, tarot cards, Ouija boards, etc.

Spirits Associated with the Stronghold of Witchcraft and Divination

Witchcraft	Marine	Fear
Divination	Serpent	Bitterness
Rebellion	Mermaid	Manipulation
Jezebel	Pagan	Fascination
Antichrist	Sorcery	Enchantment
Deception	Confusion	Seduction
Lying	Familiar	Slumber

Evicting Demons

It's clear now that the deliverance process is much more than casting out demons. Here in this segment, the time to confront and evict demons has come. The prayers during the session up to this point have removed the legal rights for any demon to remain. You've worked intensely to get here, now it's time to run to the battle like David ran to meet Goliath.

A brief prayer before the actual confrontation phase begins is helpful.

> Father, we come before you today on behalf of _____.
>
> We thank You that we can come boldly before You to the throne of grace through the blood of Jesus.
>
> We thank You that _____ has renounced and repented of all of the sins known and unknown of his ancestors, he/she has also renounced and repented of all of his / her known and unknown personal sins.
>
> We know that the blood of Jesus speaks louder than his / her sins. Therefore, we ask You to silence the voice of the Accuser. We also ask You to grant complete freedom, deliverance, and healing to _____.
>
> We declare freedom, healing and a total release of all torment, harassment, infirmity, and oppression. We forbid and bind any violent manifestation in the name of Jesus. Demons, your assignment now is to leave and be cast into the abyss in the powerful Name of Jesus.

Manifestation of Demons

Demons can manifest at any moment during the session. So, once again, team members never have their eyes closed during the session. During this phase, the team is on heightened alert.

Demon manifestations can include:

- Crying and screaming.
- Facial distortions.
- Silence and trance like states.

- Convulsions and choking.
- Hissing, growling and unnatural voices.
- Shaking and falling to the floor.
- Burping, coughing, spitting, and vomiting.
- Animal-like behavior.
- Supernatural strength.

The Manifestation Cycle

You will notice a cycle of manifestation as the demons are called up and confronted by name. This list below will help you understand what is happening:

- The person's face reflects the internal battle: fear, anxiety or discomfort are noticeable.
- Crying, coughing, and choking begins.
- The demon struggles to hold its ground verbally or physically.
- Occasionally the person becomes sleepy, silent, or catatonic.
- Screaming, burping, and spitting up.
- All the above symptoms subside resulting in a visible breakthrough.
- Relief and joy are clearly observable on the persons face when demons leave.

Remember that demons know very well how to hide to avoid detection. They will attempt to falsify the deliverance cycle. They can also resist stubbornly. They can make the person unresponsive or produce a catatonic state. There are several things we can do in this situation. Bind and break the witchcraft over the prayee. Call the person back by name. Say, "Open your eyes and look at me." Tell the prayee to fight and cooperate.

What to do in this Segment

Please note that the fruit of a stronghold is a physical manifestation such as sickness, an activity, a mindset, religion or an ideology, false religion, or witchcraft, a fleshly or sinful activity. Demons are connected to these fruits.

So, in this segment, call up the demon with the name of its fruit and cast it out with the authority of Jesus. It's very simple and you can follow these simple steps.

1. The prayee will renounce all fruit and manifestation of the stronghold being dealt with.
2. The deliverance practitioner calls up the demos and casts them out by name.

Have your chair closer to the person in this segment. After the prayer and renouncing the fruit of the stronghold, establish and maintain direct eye contact with the person as you are calling up and casting out the demons. It's very simple!

One of the key elements of deliverance is exercising the will in obedience to God and resisting the enemy. When the breakthrough is imminent and the manifestations begin to subside, be sure to enlist the prayee in the process of deliverance. Instruct the prayee to tell the demon to leave with declarations and commands like these:

- I have the blood of Jesus over me, and I belong to Him.
- I command you to leave me now in the Name of Jesus.
- I don't want you in me anymore. Leave and never return in Jesus's name.
- Get out and stay out in Jesus's name.

Blessing

It may seem unusual to say that a segment of the deliverance session is beautiful, but this one truly is. After so many years of bondage, abuse, affliction and torment, the blessing is the culmination and highlight of the entire process.

This step is simple and straightforward. Pray the prayer of blessing, feel free to improvise along the way with additional blessings as the Holy Spirit leads. Anoint the person with oil and pray for a fresh infilling of the Holy Spirit. If the prayee has not yet received the baptism of Holy Spirit with the evidence of speaking in tongues, this is the time to pray for that as well, as the Holy Spirit leads you.

> I thank God for you _____, knowing that you have humbled and opened your heart before the Lord in a deep way with absolute transparency. I thank God that He has visited you with the sweetness and power of His presence. The healing virtue of Jesus has flowed into your life and brings alignment of your past, present and future as well as your whole spirit, soul, and body with the will of God.
>
> _____, I declare that the enemy's purpose and assignment against your life has been completely canceled and deactivated. Therefore, I declare the abundant life has been released over your life.

We declare open doors and communication with the Father, Son, and Holy Spirit.
We declare a covenant of love and obedience with the Lord.
We establish God's truth in your heart to replace the darkness of the past.
We declare that new thought patterns are replacing the old now.
We decree that new cyclical patterns will usher in God's blessings in a tangible way.
We pray you will have a series of supernatural encounters with the Lord.
We declare blessings that empower your new post-deliverance life.

From this day forward:
You will experience great peace.
God will bless you with a clear understanding about your life's purpose.
You will have a heart that desires the will of God, ears that hear the voice of the Father and supernatural grace to respond quickly when He speaks to you.
You will be a blessing to many people because you are grateful for all the

Lord has done in your life.

Everything that you touch will prosper as you seek to please the Lord.

Your relationship with the Lord will grow and you will know the depth of His love for you.

You will understand the eternal principles of the Word of God and have supernatural grace to apply them to your life.

You will grow in physical health and in the joy of the Lord.

God will give you favor with man and before the heaven's throne.

The Holy Spirit will bring you into happiness in friendships with Kingdom minded people.

God will bless your family relationships with restoration and breaking down the walls of separation.

_____, I bless you with a grace to trust the Lord in times of difficulty, with wisdom to make correct decisions, with protection, provision, and strength to follow the Lord closely.

I declare that you have aligned yourself with the Kingdom of God and that you have determined to seek God's Kingdom first every day and in every decision. Therefore, I declare that the blessings of the Kingdom will follow you all the days of your life.

"The Lord bless you and keep you;
The Lord make His face shine upon you,
And be gracious to you;
The Lord lift up His countenance upon you,
And give you peace." Numbers 6:24-26

I bless you _____, in the Name of Jesus our Lord. Amen!

Homework

At this point the person is almost ready to return home after the long session. Don't allow the individual to leave without assigning the homework. We always give a copy of Silvia Sauve's book *"Be More Than a Conqueror, A Practical Guide To Walking in Freedom and Victory"* to each person after completing the session. This book is designed specifically for post-deliverance follow-up; it is packed with practical information. Consider chapter titles in the book:

1. Why should I be on guard?
2. The authority of the believer: Your authority!
3. Is your house truly clean?
4. What is the condition of your mind?
5. Are you prudent with your words?
6. Do you honor God with your finances?
7. Spiritual Discipline

Now, the person has the challenge to walk out their deliverance! Lifestyle change through a transformed mind is the desired goal of the homework. We want to facilitate the process of implementing change. Consider this: a person cannot simply continue living the same lifestyle that built strongholds and attracted demons. It took years to build the strongholds, it will now take time to restructure, regroup and rebuild a wholesome lifestyle aligned with God's will and truth.

Keep in mind, if you are married and have children at home, that the only thing that changed is you. You will need to start implementing the "new you" all around you: at home, with family members, at work, etc.

Remember that when a demon leaves, he may attempt to return to the person bringing seven others that are stronger. (Matthew 12:45) The homework is designed to edify spiritually with God's word and provoke a fresh infilling of the Holy Spirit daily.

Remind the person that there will be a follow up call.

Encourage the prayee (for today) to rest, to break the fast and spend time in the presence of the Lord. If possible, avoid social media, television, and other distractions.

The homework is:

- Read Silvia Sauve's book: *Be More Than a Conqueror* and implement the necessary changes.
- Develop a daily habit of seeking God in prayer and in His word.
- Readings from the Bible daily, at least one chapter a day.
- Remove all habits that do not lead to spiritual edification and replace them with new habits.
- Today when back at home: worship the Lord, pray and rest. Avoid social gathering or movies. Soak in the presence of God.

Before sending the person home, pray again.

- Thank God for the wonderful deliverance!
- Break any assignment of death, revenge or retaliation against the person and family.

Right after the session is completed and the prayee leaves, clean up the room where you had the session. Remove the trash and straighten up leaving everything as it was before the session. Also, you need to pray over the room where the deliverance took place. Cover the place with the Blood of Jesus. Command al lingering spirits to leave in the name of Jesus and never return.

Follow Up

The post session follow-up is very important, and it can take place one or two days after the Deliverance session. Please keep in mind that the individual has just gone through something very similar to an invasive surgery. Expect the person to be:

1. Possibly vulnerable to attack.
2. Physically tired.
3. In pain if the manifestations were intense.

The chart below can be used and shared in the follow up.

We can diagram effective and long-lasting deliverance and inner healing as follows:

75% of the outcome revolves around renewing the mind.

20% of the results comes from inner healing.

5% of the process is casting out demons!

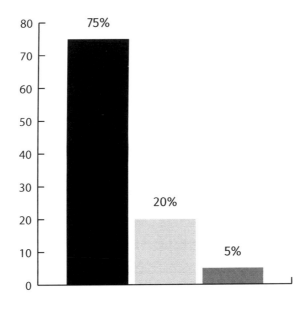

This might come as a surprise as we all tend to believe that deliverance is simply casting out demons. Darkness is being removed from the very moment a person starts the process. From the beginning of the process, the assigned reading and videos help connect the dots between action and reaction, sin and consequences, trauma, and symptoms.

The renewing of the mind starts when the process initiates and continues with the post session homework. Habits through life contributed to the building of ungodly strongholds. Now, a new lifestyle will begin to build godly strongholds with the end of solidified transformation according to the will of God.

During this follow-up session, encourage the prayee to:

1. Learn to walk in the Spirit.
2. Get involved in their church.
3. Improve their personal time of prayer and Bible reading.
4. Develops hunger and thirst for God's presence.
5. Understand that activities either build up or tear down.
6. Develop repentance as a lifestyle.
7. Build new habits that glorify the Lord.
8. Seek accountability.
9. Bring the deliverance home by cleansing the house of anything ungodly and seeking any necessary restoration and reconciliation with family members if need be and if possible.

A team member may need to follow-up with post session counseling. Use your God given skillset, knowledge, and experience to help identify any remaining open doors, weakness, vulnerability, or family situations that need to be dealt with. A broken person will have dysfunctional relationships. You may soon be ministering to the entire family. Help the individual take personal responsibility for the outcome of the session.

The team member assigned to the case can help pass the personal responsibility of their deliverance by asking questions and holding them accountable to the answers.

1. Can you clearly understand what the enemy did to you in the past?
2. Are you falling into the lifestyle of the past?
3. Do you want to stay free?
4. What are the habits that you must change?
5. What is the new lifestyle that the Lord has for you?
6. When will you begin to implement the change?
7. How can I help you?

Please remember that you are passing the responsibility of staying free and walking it out to the individual in the follow-up phase of deliverance. Emotional dependence on the deliverance team is to be avoided.

Remember that your pastor is responsible before the Lord for the members of the congregation. The team leader needs to know what type of feedback the pastor requires. We do not disclose the specifics of a prayee's life nor past sins or situations. We simply provide either a written or brief verbal report with a general result of the session.

Moving Forward

I can remember the first sessions that my wife Silvia and I led many years ago. I'm shaking my head as I think about it! Lord have mercy! We were a bit confused and disoriented in one session! Please keep in mind that love and humility will take you a long way in the Kingdom. You will learn very quickly and before you know it, much of the content of this manual will be downloaded into your spirit. The Lord does indeed have mercy, and grace. We grew into the role with practice and experience. You will, too.

There is no way to express in depth all the nuances and minute details of a deliverance session. This book might appear to be an oversimplification of the process. However, if you take this, run with it, and put into practice, your experience with the guidance of the Holy Spirit will fill in the blanks. Soon, you will have a full-fledged deliverance ministry in your church!

Please keep in mind that the preparation for this ministry is ongoing! We recommend reading books and attending seminars.

We highly recommend a degree path in Wagner University with their M.A. in Spiritual Healing, Deliverance and Warfare. There are several programs in place for Bachelor, Master's and Doctoral levels. Remember that C. Peter Wagner and his wife Doris have left a powerful legacy known around the world in evangelism, intercession, spiritual warfare, and deliverance. That same mantle and legacy continues today through the university. For more information please visit: https://wagner.university.

Those who are serious about ministering as a practitioner of deliverance and inner healing need to connect with others for peer level accountability and ongoing training to establish the credibility and importance of deliverance and inner healing. Therefore, we recommend affiliation with the International Freedom Group (IFG) which is founded by Greg and Becca Greenwood. For more information please visit: https://christianharvestintl.org.

We offer personal training and mentoring opportunities as well. The need for trained and experienced deliverance practitioners is great. Contact us and receive comprehensive, hands-on training that will equip you to help people live fulfilling lives. Please visit https://daystream.org.

Appendix A

Confidential Questionnaire

It is a requirement that the prayee fills out this Confidential Questionnaire and sends it completed to the deliverance practitioner two or more days prior to the session.

PRAYEE COMMITMENT:

- Completion of the questionnaire and any pre or post session homework.
- Willingness to forgive, repent, and maintain freedom going forward.
- To be honest and cooperative during Deliverance and Follow up session.
- To arrange for intercessors to cover him/her before and during the sessions. This is not required but is strongly recommended.
- Responsible for arrangements and cost of travel, lodging, meals, and transportation, if applicable.
- To give a donation, a suggested offering of $____ per session. In our case, we do not charge a fee but because we do have operating costs, we ask for a tax-deductible donation to our ministry.

Scheduling: upon receiving prayee's completed questionnaire, set the date and time of the deliverance session. If as an experienced practitioner you are familiar with the proper protocol, you may schedule a session via Zoom. We prefer to minister in person but sometimes that is not possible and indeed the Holy Spirit is everywhere.

INSTRUCTIONS:

Pray before filling out this questionnaire. Ask the Holy Spirit to guide you and bring critical things to your mind. The questionnaire is lengthy and VERY personal, but every question has a purpose! Please fill in everything honestly and to the best of your ability. We are not here to sit in judgement of you, but to aid in your healing process. Your privacy is of the utmost importance! We never share or discuss your personal information with anyone outside of our ministry team.

Name:　　　　　　　　　　　　　　　　**Today's date:**

Mailing address:　　　　　　　　　　**Physical address:**

Email:　　　　　　　　　　　　　　　**Mobile phone:**

Age:　　　　　　　　　　　　　　　　**Gender:**

Church you attend:

Personal Information

1. Biological gender:　Male　Female
2. Marital Status:　Married　Divorced　Single　Widow(er)
3. Maiden Name (if applicable)
4. Other names by which you've been known.
5. How did you hear about us?
6. If you were referred by your pastor / spiritual leader, list their names.
7. What is your race or ethnicity?
8. What is your sexual orientation?
9. What is your country of origin?
10. What prompted you to contact us?

This section is about you

11. How were you disciplined?
12. Describe the predominate atmosphere in your childhood home?
13. Who raised you?
14. Do you give financially (Tithes/Offerings)?　Yes　No
15. Do you have future hopes for your life?　Yes　No

Marriage and Relationships

16 Have any of your relationships been verbally, emotionally or sexually abusive?   Yes   No

17 Were any of your relationships unhealthy or toxic?   Yes   No

18 Were you raised in a Christian home?   Yes   No

19 Did you have a good relationship with your father?   Yes   No

20 Did you have a good relationship with your mother?   Yes   No

Family

21 Were you raised in an alcoholic or drug dominated home?   Yes   No

22 Do you have siblings?   Yes   No

23 Where do you fall in the sibling line?

24 Briefly describe your relationship with your siblings while you were growing up.

25 Briefly describe your relationship with your siblings today

26 Did you grow up in a happy home?   Yes   No

27 Were you a lonely child?   Yes   No

28 How would you describe your family's financial situation as a child?

29 Were you raised in a blended family?   Yes   No

30 Is (was) your father a perfectionist?   Yes   No

31 Is (was) your mother a perfectionist?   Yes   No

32 Were you raised in a verbally or physically abusive home?   Yes   No

33 Were you sexually abused at home?   Yes   No

34 Were you abused sexually outside of the home?   Yes   No

35 Are you aware of any patterns of ungodly behaviors, accidents or infirmities in your generational history?

36 Family: low income, middles class, wealthy?

37 Education Level: High School   College   Other

Career

38 What is your occupation?

39 Are you passionate and satisfied in your career?   Yes   No

40 Do you now, or have you ever had a "work spouse?"   Yes   No

41 Describe your relationship with management

42 Have you been verbally or emotionally abused at work?   Yes   No

Travel and Places Lived

43 Where have you lived?

44 Where have you traveled?

45 Have you visited pagan temples or sacred sites?

46 Do you have any cultural souvenirs from your travels?

47 Have you participated in any cultural or native ceremonies, rituals, rites?

About your birth

48 Were you a planned child?   Yes   No

49 Were you conceived out of wedlock?   Yes   No   Don't know

50 Were you adopted?   Yes   No

51 At what age were you adopted?

52 Do you know your birth parents?

53 Were either you or your mother in trauma during her pregnancy with you, or during your birth?   Yes   No   Don't know

54 Are you the sex that your parents wanted?   Yes   No   Don't know

55 Are you the sex you want to be?

56 Where were you born?

Conversion and Church Experience

57 Have you accepted Jesus and the gift of salvation?   Yes   No

58 Approximately what age did you receive salvation?

59 How has your life changed?

60 Tell us about your conversion

61 Were you baptized?   Yes   No
62 Approximately what age were you baptized?
63 In what denomination were you baptized?
64 How is your relationship with Jesus today?
65 How does the Holy Spirit communicate with you?
66 What is your church background?
67 Do you have assurance of your salvation?   Yes   No
68 Have you been filled with the Holy Spirit?   Yes   No
69 Describe the frequency of your personal devotion and prayer time?

Sexual Experience and History

70 Have you had consensual sexual contact with anyone outside of marriage?
71 Have you been raped or sexually abused?   Yes   No   Explain
72 Have you raped or sexually abused someone?   Yes   No   Explain
73 Have you been involved in prostitution?   Yes   No
74 Have you had homosexual / lesbian contact or desire?   Yes   No   Explain
75 Have you had oral or anal sex?   Yes   No
76 List names of former spouses:
77 Have you experienced sexual encounters with demons? If yes, explain:
78 Have you viewed pornography?   Yes   No   Past   Current
79 Do you frequently have lustful or sexual thoughts?   Yes   No   Past   Current
80 Have you engaged in masturbation?   Yes   No   Past   Current
81 Have you participated in Kama Sutra?   Yes   No   Past   Current
82 Have you been diagnosed with an STD?   Yes   No

Mental health

83 Are you easily frustrated? If yes, do you show it or bury it?
    Yes   No   Show   Bury
84 Would you describe yourself as: Anxious   Worrier   Depressed   N/A
85 Have you personally ever had psychiatric counselling?   Yes   No
86 Have you ever been hypnotized?   Yes   No

87 Do you ever feel mentally confused?   Yes   No

88 Do you daydream or have mental fantasies?   Yes   No

89 Do you suffer from frequent bad dreams/nightmares?   Yes   No

90 Have you ever been tempted to commit suicide?   Yes   No

91 Have you ever wished to die?   Yes   No

92 Have you ever received a mental health diagnosis?   Yes   No

93 Have you ever been diagnosed with a behavioral disorder?   Yes   No

94 To your knowledge, do you have any issues pertaining to memory loss or memory impairment?   Yes   No

Environment and Atmosphere

95 Describe the predominant atmosphere in your home

96 Do you have in your home any symbols of idols or spirit worship such as:
- ❏ None
- ❏ Totem poles
- ❏ Idol carvings
- ❏ Feathers
- ❏ Tikis
- ❏ Horoscopes
- ❏ Lucky charms
- ❏ Buddha
- ❏ Painted facemasks
- ❏ Fetish objects
- ❏ Pagan symbols
- ❏ Native art
- ❏ Astral travel
- ❏ Other

97 Do you practice feng shui?   Yes   No

98 Have you been dedicated to a god, goddess, or a saint?   Yes   No

99 Do you practice smudging?   Yes   No

100 Have you watched/read demonic movies, TV shows, magazines, websites, books?   Yes   No

101 What type of music filled your mind prior to conversion?
- ❏ Rock & Roll
- ❏ New Age
- ❏ Heavy Metal
- ❏ Gospel/Christian
- ❏ Contemporary
- ❏ Other
- ❏ Punk Rock
- ❏ Rap
- ❏ Country
- ❏ Classical
- ❏ Jazz

102 What type of music fills your mind now?
- ❑ Rock & Roll
- ❑ New Age
- ❑ Heavy Metal
- ❑ Gospel/Christian
- ❑ Contemporary
- ❑ Other
- ❑ Punk Rock
- ❑ Rap
- ❑ Country
- ❑ Classical
- ❑ Jazz

Prior Deliverance History

103 Have you ever done any deliverance ministry or inner healing ministry on yourself?

104 Have you undergone any deliverance or inner healing sessions with another ministry?

Nonsexual soul ties

105 Do you have any unhealthy emotional connections with any people, places, or objects?

Beliefs About Myself

106 My Beliefs
- ❑ I am all alone
- ❑ I am not loved, needed, cared for, or important
- ❑ I don't matter
- ❑ I am worthless with no value
- ❑ God has forsaken me
- ❑ I was a mistake
- ❑ I cannot trust anyone
- ❑ No one will believe me
- ❑ I cannot trust church leaders
- ❑ I am in the way; I am a burden
- ❑ There is no way out
- ❑ I do not know what to do
- ❑ They do not need me
- ❑ If I tell, they will come back and hurt me
- ❑ They are not coming back
- ❑ It is just a matter of time before this happens again
- ❑ I am dirty, evil, shameful, perverted, because of what happened to me

- ☐ He, she, they are coming back
- ☐ I am going to die
- ☐ I cannot stop this
- ☐ I am not acceptable
- ☐ They never liked me because I was ____!
- ☐ I couldn't do anything to please him/her
- ☐ I am so stupid ignorant, idiot
- ☐ Everything is confusing
- ☐ I will always be unclean, filthy
- ☐ I deserved it
- ☐ He/she/they are too strong to resist
- ☐ I was a participant
- ☐ He/she is going to hurt me
- ☐ I am going to die, and I cannot do anything about it
- ☐ If I trust I will die
- ☐ I am too weak to resist
- ☐ I allowed it to happen because of my looks, gender, body, etc.
- ☐ I just want to die
- ☐ I did not try to run away
- ☐ There is no way out
- ☐ I was paid for services rendered
- ☐ I am unimportant
- ☐ I kept going back
- ☐ Why would they do this to me
- ☐ I am bad, dirty, shameful, sick, nasty
- ☐ If I let him/her/them back in my life, they will hurt me
- ☐ I will always be hurt, damaged or broken because of what happened
- ☐ Something bad will happen if I tell, stop it, confront it
- ☐ I should have never been born
- ☐ I knew what was going to happen, yet I stayed away
- ☐ They do not need me
- ☐ I am just in the way
- ☐ God could never love me I was a participant
- ☐ There is no good thing for me
- ☐ I should have done something to stop it from happening
- ☐ It is never going to get any better
- ☐ It's all my fault
- ☐ It will just happen again and again
- ☐ I felt pleasure so I must have wanted it
- ☐ I have no reason to live
- ☐ I cannot get away
- ☐ I should have known better
- ☐ I am overwhelmed
- ☐ I am cheap like a slut
- ☐ Everything is out of control
- ☐ I did it to him/her first
- ☐ Not even God can help me
- ☐ I have been overlooked
- ☐ The pain is too great to bear
- ☐ No one ever really cares
- ☐ I cannot get loose

- ❏ I don't know what is happening to me
- ❏ It was all my fault
- ❏ This does not make any sense
- ❏ I should have told someone
- ❏ There are no options for me
- ❏ Doom is right around the corner
- ❏ Nothing good will ever come of this
- ❏ I should have stopped them
- ❏ No one will be able to really love me
- ❏ I don't know what to do
- ❏ My body parts are dirty
- ❏ I am pulled from every direction
- ❏ I will never be happy
- ❏ I am too small to do anything
- ❏ I will never feel clean again

Open Doors

107 Have you, your spouse, your parents, or grandparents participated in the following cults?

- ❏ Occultism
- ❏ Jehovah's Witness
- ❏ Unity
- ❏ Children of Love
- ❏ Scientology
- ❏ Communes
- ❏ Native Religions
- ❏ Islam
- ❏ Buddhism
- ❏ Mormons
- ❏ Rosicrucianism
- ❏ Gurus
- ❏ Spiritism Churches
- ❏ Christadelphians
- ❏ Bahai
- ❏ Theosophy
- ❏ Unification Church
- ❏ Hinduism
- ❏ Christian Science
- ❏ Other

108 Explain who and to what extent

109 Have you, your spouse, your parents or grandparents been a member of any of the following?

- ❏ Freemasons (lodges)
- ❏ Rainbow Girls
- ❏ Ku Klux Klan
- ❏ Job's Daughters
- ❏ Odd Fellows
- ❏ Eastern Star
- ❏ Shriners
- ❏ Daughters of the Nile

Explain who, what, when and to what extent.

110 Have you ever participated in occultism of witchcraft?   Yes   No

111 Have you participated in any of the following?

- ❏ Fortune tellers
- ❏ Ouija board
- ❏ Mediums
- ❏ Astrology
- ❏ Levitation
- ❏ Astral travel
- ❏ Black magic or magick
- ❏ White magic or magick
- ❏ Spirit guides
- ❏ Native healer
- ❏ New Age Movement
- ❏ Voodoo/Hoodoo
- ❏ None
- ❏ Tarot cards
- ❏ Seances
- ❏ Palmistry
- ❏ Color therapy
- ❏ Horoscopes
- ❏ Lucky charms
- ❏ Crystals
- ❏ Demon worship
- ❏ Automatic handwriting
- ❏ Dungeons and Dragons
- ❏ Witch Doctors
- ❏ Reiki
- ❏ Other

112 Describe your involvement with any of the above

113 Have you read books on occultism or witchcraft?   Yes   No

114 Have you made any pacts with Satan?   Yes   No

115 Do you know of any curse placed on you or your family? Yes   No

116 Have you participated in transcendental meditation?   Yes   No

117 Have you been involved in Eastern religion?   Yes   No

118 Have you practiced Yoga, Tai Chi, or Reiki?   Yes   No

119 Have you participated in telepathy or mind control?   Yes   No

120 Have you ever seen a demonic presence?   Yes   No

121 Have you participated in any of the following areas

- ❏ Familiar spirits
- ❏ Witchcraft
- ❏ Yoga
- ❏ Inferiority
- ❏ Spirit guides/animal guides
- ❏ Séances
- ❏ Racism
- ❏ Necromancy
- ❏ Other
- ❏ Divination
- ❏ Visiting mediums
- ❏ Clairvoyant
- ❏ Mind dreaming
- ❏ False prophecy
- ❏ Bigotry
- ❏ Low self-esteem
- ❏ Self-pity
- ❏ Drugs: illegal or prolonged legal use

122 Have you ever participated in any of the following areas?

- ❏ Divination
- ❏ Fortune telling or soothsayers
- ❏ Hypnotist-enchanter
- ❏ Acupuncture
- ❏ Magic (Black or White)
- ❏ Self-will
- ❏ Warlock
- ❏ Sorcerer
- ❏ Spirit guides
- ❏ Animal guides
- ❏ Water witching
- ❏ Lust for power and control
- ❏ False prophecy
- ❏ Rebellion
- ❏ Stargazing, zodiac, horoscopes
- ❏ Birth charts
- ❏ Spiritism
- ❏ Mind control / manipulation
- ❏ Witches
- ❏ Wizard
- ❏ Vampires
- ❏ Astral projection
- ❏ Ghosts
- ❏ Other

123 Have you learned martial arts?   Yes   No

124 Have you ever had premonitions, Déjà vu, or Psychic sight?   Yes   No

125 Do (did) either of your parents suffer from depression?   Yes   No

126 Are you experiencing problems in any of the following areas?

- ❏ Fear
- ❏ Fear of death
- ❏ Stress
- ❏ Depression
- ❏ Fear of saying no
- ❏ Lack of trust
- ❏ Worry
- ❏ Fear of abandonment
- ❏ Fear of authority
- ❏ Fear of heights
- ❏ Panic attacks
- ❏ Constant desire to be alone
- ❏ Fear of animals
- ❏ Fear of not being good enough
- ❏ Torment - Horror
- ❏ Anxiety
- ❏ Extrovert
- ❏ Desire to be hermit or recluse
- ❏ Migraines
- ❏ Doubt
- ❏ Fear of rejection
- ❏ Fear of heart attacks
- ❏ Fear of failure
- ❏ A critical spirit
- ❏ Unhealthy fear of God
- ❏ Fear of spiders
- ❏ Fear of others
- ❏ Other

127 In your Christian experience do you:
- ❑ Have trouble accepting the deity of Christ
- ❑ Tend to often be in heretical teaching
- ❑ Tend to gravitate toward humanistic teaching
- ❑ Have trouble accepting God's forgiveness
- ❑ Not believe you have an anointing on your life
- ❑ Tend to have a lawlessness about you
- ❑ Have trouble accepting Christ's atoning sacrifice
- ❑ Seem to be always be persecuted in your walk with Christ
- ❑ Other

128 Are you currently experiencing problems in any of the following areas?
- ❑ Lust
- ❑ Spiritual deadness
- ❑ Bitterness
- ❑ Oppression
- ❑ My ambitions / achievements
- ❑ Religion
- ❑ Compulsive behavior
- ❑ Ungodly lifestyle
- ❑ Satanic interest
- ❑ Fear of death
- ❑ Various forms of corruption
- ❑ A bound mind
- ❑ Control over your life
- ❑ Spiritual blindness
- ❑ Addictions
- ❑ Bitterness and unforgiveness

129 Have you ever used any of the following drugs?
- ❑ LSD
- ❑ Marijuana
- ❑ Crack
- ❑ Downers
- ❑ Speed
- ❑ Cocaine
- ❑ Uppers
- ❑ Other illegal street drugs

130 Are you addicted to any of the following
- ❑ Gambling
- ❑ Alcohol
- ❑ Compulsive exercise
- ❑ Coffee
- ❑ Pornography
- ❑ Drugs (Rx or illegal)
- ❑ Television
- ❑ Smoking
- ❑ Food
- ❑ Shopping
- ❑ Sex
- ❑ Other

131 Have you ever been a member of a gang?   Yes   No

132 Are you currently experiencing problems in any of the following areas?

- ❏ Mental illness
- ❏ Near drowning
- ❏ Spiritual blindness or deafness
- ❏ Alzheimer's
- ❏ Gnashing of teeth
- ❏ Burned
- ❏ Prostration
- ❏ Self-mutilation
- ❏ Insanity
- ❏ Senility
- ❏ Seizures
- ❏ Paranoia
- ❏ Hallucinations
- ❏ Attention deficit
- ❏ Ear problems
- ❏ Crippled
- ❏ Foaming at the mouth
- ❏ Excessive crying or tearing
- ❏ Pining away
- ❏ Chemical imbalance
- ❏ Suicidal
- ❏ Madness
- ❏ Retardation
- ❏ Schizophrenia
- ❏ Epilepsy
- ❏ Hearing voices
- ❏ Palsy
- ❏ Eating disorders

133 Are you currently experiencing problems in any of the following areas?

- ❏ Error in doctrine
- ❏ An unsubmissive attitude
- ❏ Twisting of scripture
- ❏ Defensive / argumentative
- ❏ New age movement
- ❏ Servant of corruption
- ❏ Fears
- ❏ Hindrance to prayer

- ❏ Hindrance to Holy Spirit moves
- ❏ Hindrance to Bible study
- ❏ False doctrines such as:
  Mormonism,
  Catholicism, Buddhism,
  Hinduism, Unitarianism
- ❏ False prophecy
- ❏ Hyper spirituality
- ❏ Unteachable spirit
- ❏ Mixture of holy and profane
- ❏ Contentiousness
- ❏ Mental confusion
- ❏ Maintaining a form of godliness
- ❏ Hindrances to hearing sermons
  Hindrance to believing
- ❏ faith principles
- ❏ Dullness of comprehension
- ❏ Other

134 Are you currently experiencing problems in any of the following areas?

- ❏ Haughtiness
- ❏ Scornful pride
- ❏ Professional pride
- ❏ Obstinate
- ❏ Self-righteous
- ❏ Manipulative
- ❏ Overbearing or domineering
- ❏ Gossip
- ❏ Exalted feelings
- ❏ Rejection of man's authority
- ❏ Contentiousness
- ❏ Strife
- ❏ Performance orientation
- ❏ Attention seeking
- ❏ Always right
- ❏ Arrogant and smug
- ❏ Religious pride
- ❏ Vanity
- ❏ Regional pride
- ❏ National pride
- ❏ Sexual pride
- ❏ Dictatorial and controlling
- ❏ Rebellion
- ❏ Impatience
- ❏ Rejection of God's authority
- ❏ Egotistical
- ❏ Self-deception
- ❏ Holier than thou attitude
- ❏ Idleness
- ❏ Bragging and boastful attitude
- ❏ Interrupting others
- ❏ Other

135 Did either of your parents suffer from depression?   Yes   No

136 Are you experiencing problems in any of the following areas?

- ❏ Self-hate
- ❏ Many regrets
- ❏ Life's unfairness
- ❏ Suicidal thoughts
- ❏ Gluttony
- ❏ Dejection
- ❏ Discouragement
- ❏ Hopelessness
- ❏ Rejection
- ❏ Abandonment
- ❏ Insomnia
- ❏ Suppressed emotions
- ❏ Self-pity
- ❏ A broken heart
- ❏ Depression
- ❏ Excessive mourning
- ❏ Loneliness
- ❏ Inner hurts and a torn spirit
- ❏ Despair
- ❏ Inferiority
- ❏ Insecurity
- ❏ Low self-esteem
- ❏ False responsibility
- ❏ Continuous sorrow and grief

137 Do you use Marijuana?   Yes   No

138 List any prescription medication you currently take that alters your mental state or your behaviors (such as opioids, anti-depressants, stimulants, etc.)

139 Have you had any major accidents requiring medical attention? (list with age)

140 Have you had any near drowning experiences?   Yes   No

141 Have you had any near-death experiences?   Yes   No

142 Are you experiencing problems in any of the following areas?

- ❏ Circulatory (blood)
- ❏ Respiratory (breathing)
- ❏ Digestive
- ❏ Endocrine (hormones)
- ❏ Nervous system
- ❏ Excretory system
- ❏ Reproductive
- ❏ Lymphatic
- ❏ Other
- ❏ Skeletal
- ❏ Muscular
- ❏ Immune system
- ❏ Allergies: seasonal, food, etc
- ❏ Chronic pain
- ❏ Undiagnosed issues
- ❏ Migraines
- ❏ Fibromyalgia

143 Please list any medical diagnosis related to the above.

144 Have you experienced any major illness or condition not listed above? (viral, bacterial, infections, etc.)   Yes   No

145 Have you had any plastic surgery? If yes, describe.

146 What other surgeries have you had?

147 Have you had a blood transfusion?   Yes   No

148 Have either your birth parents, adoptive parents, grandparents, great grandparents experienced issues with any of the following?

- ❏ Circulatory (blood)
- ❏ Respiratory (breathing)
- ❏ Digestive
- ❏ Endocrine (hormones)
- ❏ Nervous system
- ❏ Excretory system
- ❏ Reproductive
- ❏ Lymphatic
- ❏ Other
- ❏ Skeletal
- ❏ Muscular
- ❏ Immune system
- ❏ Allergies: seasonal, food, etc
- ❏ Chronic pain
- ❏ Undiagnosed issues
- ❏ Migraines
- ❏ Fibromyalgia

149 Are you currently experiencing problems in any of the following areas?

- ❏ Jealousy
- ❏ Spite
- ❏ Extreme competition
- ❏ Coveting
- ❏ Envy
- ❏ Contentiousness
- ❏ Anger and rage
- ❏ Bigotry and racism
- ❏ Suppressed rage
- ❏ Revenge
- ❏ Cruelty
- ❏ Causing divisions
- ❏ Selfishness
- ❏ Strife
- ❏ Hatred
- ❏ Violence
- ❏ Suppressed anger
- ❏ Desire to murder

150 Are you currently experiencing problems in any of the following areas?

- ❏ Lying
- ❏ Driving zeal
- ❏ False prophecy
- ❏ Exaggeration
- ❏ Slander
- ❏ Religious bondage
- ❏ Superstitions
- ❏ Guilt
- ❏ Condemnation
- ❏ Self-deception
- ❏ Frenzied emotional actions
- ❏ Flattery
- ❏ Strong deception
- ❏ Gossip
- ❏ False teaching
- ❏ Accusations
- ❏ Covenant breaking
- ❏ Profanity
- ❏ Shame
- ❏ Melancholy nature
- ❏ False burdens

151 Have you participated in, or are you currently experiencing any of the following?

- ❏ Perversity
- ❏ Evil actions
- ❏ Child abuse
- ❏ Masturbation
- ❏ A filthy mind
- ❏ Doctrinal error
- ❏ Molestation
- ❏ Rape
- ❏ Broken spirit
- ❏ Past abortions
- ❏ Prostitution
- ❏ Atheism
- ❏ Sexual perversions
- ❏ Twisting the word
- ❏ Incest
- ❏ Date rape

- ❏ Spousal rape
- ❏ Chronic worrier
- ❏ Contentious
- ❏ Lust
- ❏ Lesbianism
- ❏ Rebellion
- ❏ Emotional frigidity
- ❏ Masculine spirit (women)
- ❏ Adultery
- ❏ Pornography
- ❏ Self-lover
- ❏ Foolishness
- ❏ Homosexuality
- ❏ Vain imaginations
- ❏ Sexual frigidity
- ❏ Effeminate spirit (men)
- ❏ Fornication

152 Have you participated in, or are you currently experiencing any of the following?

- ❏ Addiction to entertainment
- ❏ Love of money
- ❏ Excessive masturbation
- ❏ Idolatry
- ❏ Love of self
- ❏ Addiction to sports
- ❏ Prostitution: spirit, soul, body
- ❏ Unfaithfulness
- ❏ Excessive appetite
- ❏ Worldliness
- ❏ Chronic dissatisfaction
- ❏ Self-reward
- ❏ Addiction to television

153 Do you have any tattoos?   Yes   No

154 Are you currently experiencing problems in any of the following areas?

- ❏ Seducing spirits
- ❏ Deception
- ❏ Seducers and enticers
- ❏ Wander from the truth
- ❏ Fascination with evil people
- ❏ Attracted to false prophets
- ❏ Jezebel (control)
- ❏ Seared conscience
- ❏ Fascination with evil ways
- ❏ Fascination with evil objects
- ❏ Hypocritical lies
- ❏ Attracted to false signs
- ❏ Attracted to false wonders
- ❏ Ahab spirit (passivity)

155 Are you experiencing problems in any of the following areas?

- ❏ Death seems to lurk nearby
- ❏ Suicide
- ❏ Fighting
- ❏ Speeding
- ❏ Disease
- ❏ Clumsiness
- ❏ Dare devil acts
- ❏ Death to marriage

- ❏ Death to relationships
- ❏ Accidents
- ❏ Death wish
- ❏ Death to ministry
- ❏ Random acts of violence

156 Are you experiencing problems in any of the following areas?

- ❏ ADD, ADHD
- ❏ Blind
- ❏ Confusion
- ❏ Distracted easily
- ❏ Fear
- ❏ Lethargy
- ❏ Perversions
- ❏ Arthritis
- ❏ Circulatory problems
- ❏ Eye disorders
- ❏ Palpitations
- ❏ Sleeplessness
- ❏ Torment
- ❏ Blasphemer
- ❏ Can't hear the word of God
- ❏ Can't stay awake in church
- ❏ Dizziness
- ❏ Lazy
- ❏ Mental slowness
- ❏ Anemia
- ❏ Asthma
- ❏ Chronic fatigue syndrome
- ❏ Hearing problems
- ❏ Sleepiness
- ❏ Terror
- ❏ Unbelief

157 Are you experiencing problems in any of the following areas?

- ❏ Legalism
- ❏ Pride
- ❏ Holier-than-thou attitude
- ❏ Ritual over relationship
- ❏ Slumber
- ❏ Bondage
- ❏ Fear
- ❏ Against the moves of God
- ❏ Fear of what others think
- ❏ Must do and say the right thing
- ❏ Condemnation of others
- ❏ Unbelief
- ❏ Fear of failure
- ❏ Self-exalting
- ❏ Steeped in tradition
- ❏ Speaks against moves of God
- ❏ Superstition
- ❏ Ritual
- ❏ Rigid dogma
- ❏ No room for gifts of Holy Spirit
- ❏ Idol worship
- ❏ Spiritually dead
- ❏ No thriving relationship with Jesus
- ❏ Intellectualism
- ❏ Cannot relate to supernatural
- ❏ Places God in a box

- ❏ Judgmental
- ❏ Prideful
- ❏ Self-righteous
- ❏ Deception
- ❏ Righteousness through works

158 Are you experiencing problems in any of the following areas?

- ❏ Appearing prophetic
- ❏ Seeks favor of leaders
- ❏ Usurps authority
- ❏ Pride
- ❏ Seduction by words or actions
- ❏ Manipulation
- ❏ Looks for the weak link
- ❏ Quick to find fault
- ❏ Impure motive
- ❏ Secretive in prayer
- ❏ Uses evil deeds to control
- ❏ Financial greed
- ❏ False humility
- ❏ Threatened by true prophets
- ❏ Seeks weakness in others
- ❏ Takes control
- ❏ Control
- ❏ Seeks endorsement
- ❏ Seeks recognition
- ❏ Uses flattery
- ❏ Doctrinal error
- ❏ Seeks to lead disciples
- ❏ Occult involvement
- ❏ Sexual perversion
- ❏ Illegal wealth building
- ❏ Demonstrative spiritual actions

159 Have you or your ancestors experienced problems in any of the following areas?

- ❏ Cycles of misery
- ❏ Ignorance
- ❏ Destitution
- ❏ Spiritual blindness
- ❏ Intellectual blindness
- ❏ Laziness
- ❏ Boredom
- ❏ Apathy
- ❏ Entitlement
- ❏ Fear of the future
- ❏ Seeking peer approval
- ❏ Temporal satisfaction
- ❏ Pride
- ❏ Depression
- ❏ Rebellion
- ❏ Poverty and lack
- ❏ Rejecting God
- ❏ Shame
- ❏ Blame shifting
- ❏ Injustice

160 Is there anything else you think we should know?

161 What do you hope to receive from the Lord by going through this deliverance process?

162 What are your dreams for the future?

This questionnaire is provided by Jareb and Petra Nott, adapted and used with permission. www.edt.training, www.christianharvestintl.org

Appendix B

Request and Consent to Receive In-Depth Personal Ministry

Name
Address
Phone
Reasons for Requesting Ministry

Instructions

1. (Minister's name) is neither a psychotherapist, mental health professional nor a psychologist. This is a Holy Spirit and Bible based prayer ministry. The process may take several hours. Be prepared for an appointment of this length.

2. Pray before you begin to fill out the questionnaire. Ask the Holy Spirit to help and guide you and bring key things to your mind. Please add any additional information concerning issues that may shed light on situations that produced trauma, great disappointment or hurt. Names may be requested for ministry purposes only – first names only. You must be ready and willing to forgive all who have sinned against you for good results. Forgiveness is a great weapon to disarm the enemy.

3. Full disclosure and complete honesty are required. If you are unwilling to comply or to forgive, when necessary, please wait and reschedule when you are ready. Results will not be satisfactory and may even be hurtful in the long run if we are unable to minister in depth and your complete honesty. Confidentiality will be maintained. Be assured that "We have heard

it all" and nothing will shock or anger us. We are here to aid in the healing process.

4. If you are physically able, please consider a special time to pray and fast before your appointment. If you have mature Christian friends who are aware of your appointment, consider asking them to join you in prayer and fasting. This adds strength, guidance effectiveness to the process.

5. If your problem is about sin, past or present, we will minister to you only if you are willing to forsake such behavior and cut it off. Be warned that if a person invites the problem back, the latter state may be far worse that the original and much effort, time and energy will have been wasted. You must agree to this or reschedule for a later date.

6. We (Ministry name, prayer ministry name) do not charge for this ministry. However, there is a suggested donation of $_____ per session. We do have operating costs, and therefore we ask for a donation to our ministry.

7. Please return this questionnaire to:

I have read the above instructions and agree to comply fully.

Name   Date

Voluntary Release, Assumption of Risk, and Indemnity Agreement

In consideration for being permitted to participate in a voluntary prayer ministry, herein referred to as the "Prayer Ministry", the undersigned, _____, herein referred to as the "Releaser", agrees as follows:

1. RELEASE, WAIVER, DISCHARGE AND COVENANT NOT TO SUE: Releasor and releasor's personal representatives, insurers, heirs, executors, administrators, spouse, and next of kin hereby releases, waives, discharges and covenants not to sue (Prayer Ministry name, Minister's name), and it's directors, officers, employees, agents, volunteers, as well as it's successors, all herein referred to as "Releasees", from any liability to Releaser and to releasor's personal representatives, insurers, heirs, executors, administrators, spouse, and next of kin for any and all loss, damage, or cost on account of injury to the person or property or resulting in the death

of Releasor, whether caused by the negligence of Releasees or otherwise with Releasor is participating in the Prayer Ministry and any other activities in connecting with the Prayer Ministry.

2. ASSUMPTION OF RISK. Releasor understands, is aware of, and assumes all risks inherent in participating in the Prayer Ministry. These risks include but are not limited to, physical and emotional responses and reactions as a result of this prayer ministry.

3. INDEMNITY. Releasor agrees to indemnify Releasees from any liability, loss, damage, or cost that may be incurred due to the participation by Releasor in the Prayer Ministry whether caused by negligence or otherwise. Releasor assumes full responsibility for and risk of bodily injury, death, or property damage due to the negligence of Releasees or otherwise while participating in this Prayer Ministry.

Releasor expressly agrees that this Voluntary Release, Assumption of Risk, and Indemnity Agreement, herein referred to as "Agreement", is intended to be as broad and inclusive as permitted by the State of (_____) and that, if any portion of this Agreement is held invalid, it is agreed that a balance, notwithstanding, continues in full force and effect. This Agreement contains the entire agreement between parties in regard to the Prayer Ministry.

RELEASOR REPRESENTS THAT:

I HAVE CAREFULLY READ THIS AGREEMENT. I UNDERSTAND THAT IT IS A RELEASE OF ALL CLAIMS, INCLUDING THE NEGLIGENCE OF RELEASEES.

I UNDERSTAND THAT I ASSUME ALL RISKS INHERENT IN THE PRAYER MINISTRY SET FORTH IN THIS AGREEMENT.

I UNDERSTAND THAT I AM INDEMNIFYING THE RELEASEES.

I VOLUNTARILY SIGN MY NAME EVIDENCING MY UNDERSTANDING AND ACCEPTANCE OF THE PROVISIONS OF THIS AGREEMENT.

_____   _____
DATE   Signature of Releasor

This form is provided by and used with permission of Doris Wagner.

Appendix C

Deliverance Preparation Checklist

This list is designed to help you keep track of each individual seeking deliverance. Using this list will remove any doubt about the individual's progress in personal preparation and enable you to schedule the session date.

Name:

Date requested deliverance:
- ☐ Deliverance is needed
- ☐ Pastor approves prayee for personal deliverance ministry
- ☐ Read required materials
- ☐ Watched the required videos
- ☐ Read *Deliverance on Purpose*
- ☐ Sent the Confidential Questionnaire
- ☐ Session date scheduled
- ☐ Interview after completed Questionnaire
- ☐ Prayers to renounce: Islam, Freemasonry, Catholicism

Appendix D

The Session Checklist

The session checklist is designed to be a quick reference guide to ensure that all areas of the process have been addressed.

- ❑ Warm up
- ❑ Deliverance Prayer
- ❑ Forgiveness and Inner Healing
- ❑ Breaking Soul Ties
- ❑ Terminating Generational Curses
- ❑ Revoking Agreement with Darkness
- ❑ Demolishing Strongholds and Evicting Demons
- ❑ Blessing
- ❑ Homework
- ❑ Clean up

Appendix E

Additional Prayers of Release

Spiritual "Bolt-Cutter" Prayer

Occasionally there are moments in a session when the prayee shuts down and no longer wishes to cooperate or continue with the process. Consider the content of this prayer and gently lead the prayee out of the impasse.

> Dear Heavenly Father:
>
> I come to You in the name of the Lord Jesus Christ. And I renounce and turn from all lies, all preconceptions, deceptions, and self-deceptions, and all unteachableness that I or my ancestors have believed or entertained.
>
> I confess them as my sins and I ask to be cleansed from them by the Blood of the Lord Jesus Christ. I renounce all vows of secrecy and silence about all ungodly activities.
>
> I command every lying spirit, and every spirit of deception, self-deception, and unteachableness, and any other spirits associated with these sins to leave me now, harmlessly on my natural breathing, and not to return to me or to anyone whom I love, in the Name of the Lord Jesus Christ.
>
> In the name of the Lord Jesus Christ, I come out of agreement with and renounce all shame, blame and guilt, all fear, all fear of failure, all fear of rejection, all fear of men, all fear of offending and ridicule, and all fear of not hearing God.
>
> Lord Jesus, you are the Truth, and I surrender all these areas to Your Holy Spirit, who is the Spirit of Truth, and whom You promised would lead me into all truth. In Jesus' Name. Amen.

Prayer of renunciation and release for those previously involved in the Church of Jesus Christ of the Latter-day Saints.

Please pause briefly following each paragraph to allow the Holy Spirit to show any additional issues that He may wish to bring to your attention.

"Father God, creator of the heavens and the earth, I come to you in the name of Jesus Christ your Son. I come as a sinner seeking forgiveness and cleansing from all sins I have committed against you, and against all others made in your image. I honor my earthly father and mother, and all of my ancestors of flesh and blood, and of the spirit by adoption, but I utterly turn away from and renounce all their sins. I forgive all in my family line for the effects of their sins on me and my children. I confess and renounce all of my own sins. I renounce and rebuke Satan and every power of his affecting me and my family.

In the name of Jesus Christ, I renounce every action and word of mine which gave others permission to deceive and control me. I renounce, forsake and break every covenant I have ever made with the Church of Jesus Christ of the Latter-day Saints. I renounce and forsake the false headship and authority of the President and the General Authorities, all Quorum of the Twelve Apostles; all members of the Presidency of the Seventy; all members of the Second Quorum of the Seventy; and all Presiding Bishoprics; and their idolatrous usurping of their organization in the place of the Lord Jesus Christ.

In the name of Jesus Christ, I renounce and forsake the heretical writings of Joseph Smith Jnr; Brigham Young; all Presidents, all General Authorities, and all other writings published by the Church of Jesus Christ of Latter-day Saints. Lord Jesus, help me to honor you by removing all these books and publications from my home and life, and I cut off every bondage I have been under because of those writings, in the name of Jesus Christ.

In the name of Jesus Christ I renounce and cut off my life the ungodly Covenants of Baptism and Membership of the Church of Jesus Christ of Latter-day Saints; including all false Aaronic and Melchizedek Priesthoods, and all the witchcraft and Masonic oaths invoked in those initiation ceremonies. I renounce these and all other ungodly soul ties, and I command the spirits that empower those soul ties to leave me now in the name of Jesus Christ. I gather those soul ties together and sever them through with the Sword of the Spirit of God, and humbly request the blood of Jesus Christ to seal those ends so they will never be able to reconnect.

Lord Jesus, you are the wonderful Counselor, and you know all my problems, all those things that bind, torment, defile and harass me. I now confess that my body is the temple of the Holy Spirit, redeemed, cleansed and sanctified by the blood of Jesus Christ.

I ask you, Lord Jesus, to fill me now with your Holy Spirit, so that He will give me insight and understanding when I read and study your Word. I enthrone you, Lord Jesus in my heart, for you are my Lord and Savior, the source of eternal life. Thank you, Father God, for your mercy, your forgiveness and your love, in the name of Jesus Christ. Amen."

Prayer of renunciation and release for those previously involved in the Watchtower Society/Jehovah's Witnesses

Please pause briefly following each paragraph to allow the Holy Spirit to show any additional issues which He may wish to bring to your attention.

"Father God, creator of the heavens and the earth, I come to you in the name of Jesus Christ your Son. I choose to accept the sacrifice made by Jesus at Calvary for me to pay for my sins and iniquities. I come as a sinner seeking forgiveness and cleansing from all sins I have committed against you, and against all others made in your image. I honor my earthly father and mother, and all of my ancestors of flesh and blood, and of the spirit by adoption, but I utterly turn away from and renounce all their sins. I forgive all in my family line for the effects of their sins on me and my children. I confess and renounce all of my own sins. I renounce and rebuke Satan and every power of his affecting me and my family.

In the name of the Lord Jesus Christ, I renounce every action and word of mine which gave others permission to deceive and control me. I renounce, forsake and break every covenant I have ever made with the Watchtower Society of Jehovah's Witnesses. I renounce and forsake the false headship and authority of the President and the Governing Body of the Watchtower Society, and their idolatrous usurping of their organization in the place of the Lord Jesus Christ.

In the name of Jesus Christ, I renounce and forsake the heretical writings of Charles Taze Russell, Joseph Rutherford, Nathan Knorr, Frederick Franz, Milton Henchel, and all other writings published by the Watchtower Society. Lord Jesus, help me to honor you by removing all these books and publications from my home and life, and I cut off every bondage I have been under because of those writings, in the name of Jesus Christ.

In the name of Jesus Christ I renounce and cut off my life the ungodly Covenants of Baptism and Membership of the Jehovah's Witnesses; I renounce these and all other ungodly soul ties, and I command the spirits that empower those

Additional Prayers of Release

soul ties to leave me now in the name of Jesus Christ. I gather those soul ties together and sever them through with the Sword of the Spirit of God, and humbly request the blood of Jesus Christ to seal those ends so they will never be able to reconnect.

Holy Spirit, given by my savior Jesus Christ as my wonderful teacher, counselor, and revealer of God's Word, (the Bible) I confess and apologise for accepting the false teaching and belief that you are not Deity but only the power of God like electricity. Please forgive me, and do not hold me guilty of the only unforgiveable sin, namely blaspheming the Holy Spirit, as stated by Jesus Christ and as shown in Matthew chapter 12 verses 31 & 32. You know all my problems, all those things that bind, torment, defile and harass me. I now confess that my body is the temple of the Holy Spirit, redeemed, cleansed and sanctified by the blood of Jesus Christ.

I ask you, Lord Jesus, to fill me now with your Holy Spirit, so that He will give me insight and understanding when I read and study your Word. I enthrone you, Lord Jesus in my heart, for you are my Lord and Savior, the source of eternal life. Thank you, Father God, for your mercy, your forgiveness and your love, in the name of Jesus Christ. Amen."

Acknowledgement is given to Selwyn Stevens at Jubilee Resources for providing these prayers. https://jubileeresources.org

Appendix F

Building a Team

Background Information

The central focus of this manual is the deliverance process and session. Every phase is essential for effective ministry. As a backdrop for the process let's look briefly at the deliverance team protocols and team building requirements.

The Deliverance Team

We understand clearly that Jesus never changes and that His character, power, intentional love and desire to save, heal and deliver will never change. Jesus is the same today, yesterday and forever! (Hebrews 13:8) With this in mind, we must remember that Jesus came to destroy the works of the devil (1 John 3:8) and that this mission is now carried out by His disciples. Working together as a team increases effectiveness because it promotes power through agreement as well as insures transparency.

As general protocols deliverance team members must...

- Be emotionally and spiritually mature.
- Demonstrate humility and a teachable spirit.
- Have an up-to-date relationship with the Lord, walking in faith and in holiness.
- Personal prayer and fasting are considered standard operating procedure.
- Have sound biblical understanding.
- Desire to serve.

- Desire to learn and personally apply acquired revelation.
- Operate under delegated authority. All members must have an apostolic authority over their life. Who are the team members accountable to?

For the session...

- Work in teams. Jesus sent His disciples out two at a time – never initiate a session alone!
  - Preferably, the team should have both men and women so there will never be two men ministering to one woman, or two women ministering to one man.
- Have a designated leader responsible for the direction of the session
- Pray together before the session to ask for guidance of the Lord and to establish unity and agreement.
- Others can be in a supportive role. They are to pray quietly in the Spirit and learn.
- Respect the person seeking deliverance with absolute confidentiality of whatever happens in the sessions.
- Anticipate possible strong physical manifestations and prepare the room accordingly.
- Keep physical touch to a minimum for those seeking deliverance since many have been abused or have issues with mistrust.
- Keep in mind that screaming and yelling does not increase anointing or authority; on the contrary, it may increase the fear factor for those seeking deliverance.

The Deliverance Team Building Process

There is a process in the development of the team. This process is on an individual and a team level. Interview each potential team member and ask appropriate questions such as:

1. Why do you want to be part of the deliverance team?

2. Have you had experience in counseling or deliverance?
3. Are you committed and under authority in this church?
4. (If married) Is your spouse in agreement with you becoming a member of the team?
5. Have you been through the deliverance process yourself?
6. Can you guard in absolute confidentiality what is shared and happens in a session?
7. Are you willing to grow spiritually and continue to learn?

The team has a cycle of growth and development.

1. Selection of team members.
2. Training team members the basic foundations of deliverance ministry
3. Completing a personal deliverance session with each member.
4. Fine-tuning personality and relationship issues among the members.
5. Facilitating for members to have practical and hands on experience during a session (guided by leaders).
6. Guided release: each member will lead a session with the support of the team leader.
7. Full release: members move on to minister deliverance under delegated authority.

Please keep in mind that the preparation for this ministry is ongoing! We recommend reading books and attending seminars to glean helpful information.

We also recommend that the Team Leader, in addition to an apostolic covering, seek mentoring from a recognized deliverance minister.

There comes the time for the eaglets to fly. They may still want the safety of the nest! The experienced team leader will encourage them to fly and help with follow-up after the solo flight sessions.

DayStream Information and Tools

Please don't hesitate to contact us if you have any questions or concerns. We would be honored to help you begin your deliverance ministry.

Upon request we can provide the following prayers and files in digital format:

1. The Confidential Questionnaire
2. The Deliverance Preparation Checklist
3. The Session Checklist

Address:

DayStream Ministries International
P. O. Box 5261
Lighthouse Point, FL 33074

Emails:

silvia@daystream.org
ernie@daystream.org

Websites:

English: http://daystream.org
Spanish: https://liberacionenjesus.com

Office Phone:

+1-954 – 512 – 7275

Books and Online Courses – English

Deliverance on Purpose – Power Principles that Unlock your Destiny

Dr. Ernie Sauve Jr.

Be More than a Conqueror – A Practical Guide to Walking in Freedom and Victory

Silvia Sauve

Online Courses

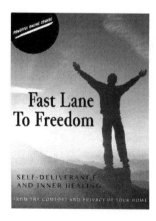

Fast Lane to Freedom

This powerful **ONLINE** course will guide you through an exciting journey of self-deliverance and inner healing!

The *Freedom School of Deliverance BOOT CAMP* is the second step in your training to serve the Lord effectively as a competent deliverance minister. The first step was successfully completing our Fast Lane to Freedom online course.

Books and Online Courses – Spanish

Liberación Intencional – Principios Poderosos que Desatan tu Destino

Dr. Ernesto Sauve Jr.

¡Sé más que Vencedor! Guía práctica para caminar libre y victorioso

Silvia Sauve

Cursos en Línea

¡Libres para Volar!

¡Este poderoso curso EN LÍNEA te guiará a través de un emocionante viaje de auto liberación y sanidad interior!

For a complete listing of our materials and products please visit:

https://daystream.org/store

Made in the USA
Columbia, SC
08 July 2024